the christmas

collection

First published in 1998
by Hamlyn
an imprint of Reed Consumer Books Limited
Michelin House, 81 Fulham Road, London SW3 6RB
and Auckland, Melbourne, Singapore and Toronto

ISBN: 0-600-59644-3

Printed in China

Notes
Eggs should be medium unless otherwise stated.

The Department of Health advises that eggs should not be consumed raw.
This book contains dishes made with raw or lightly cooked eggs. It is prudent
for pregnant women, nursing mothers, invalids, the elderly, babies and young
children to avoid uncooked or lightly cooked dishes made with eggs. Once
prepared, these dishes should be kept refrigerated and used promptly.

Milk should be full fat unless otherwise stated.

Nuts and Nut Derivatives This book includes dishes made with nuts and nut
derivatives. It is advisable for those with known allergic reactions to nuts and
nut derivatives and anyone potentially vulnerable to these allergies, including
pregnant and nursing mothers, invalids, the elderly, babies and children to
avoid dishes made with nuts and nut oils. It is also wise to check the labels
of pre-prepared ingredients for the possible inclusion of nuts.

Ovens should be heated to the specified temperature – if using a fan-assisted
oven, follow the manufacturer's instructions for adjusting the cooking time
and temperature.

Standard level spoon measurements are used in all recipes.
1 tablespoon = one 15ml spoon
1 teaspoon = one 5ml spoon

contents

introduction

Christmas is a time for celebration, a time to reunite with friends and to gather the family together. Wherever you are in the world, this invariably involves feasting and there are many foods traditionally eaten during Christmas and the festive season. Although many of these traditions are ancient and steeped in legend, they are often still observed today, making them fascinating and delicious, relics of the past. Desserts, cakes and pastries are particularly popular around Christmas and families all over the world bake tempting sweetmeats with which to treat the family, greet unexpected guests and even carol singers, and to give as lovingly prepared gifts to their friends and neighbours.

Wherever in the world these desserts originate from, they usually contain the same rich ingredients, probably because they were all that was on offer at this lean time of year. They include nuts such as Brazils, pecans, almonds, hazelnuts, walnuts and chestnuts, often used ground in pastes such as marzipan, or in mincemeat used to fill mince pies. Dried fruits such as currants, raisins, dates and prunes and crystallised citrus peel are also often found in Christmas desserts from all over the world, as are fresh fruits that can be stored from the autumn, such as apples and pears. Desserts are usually sweetened with treacle or honey, regarded in ancient times as the food of the gods and a symbol of wealth and happiness. The last ingredients common to many Christmas foods are spices. Ginger, cinnamon, cloves, nutmeg and cardamom are common, making traditional Christmas desserts burst with exotic flavours, perfect for the most important celebration of the year.

Christmas Foods

Christmas cake A rich fruit cake, doused with alcohol, wrapped in marzipan and iced with royal icing, makes a decorative centrepiece for a Christmas tea table. There are endless ways of decorating a Christmas cake, with patterns in the icing, coloured marzipan shapes and figures, crystallised fruits and peel or whole nuts. Most countries have their own traditional Christmas cake. For example, in Italy, it is panettone, a sweet bread enriched with egg yolks and containing raisins and dried peel, topped with a dusting of icing sugar. The German version is stollen, a yeasted fruit cake, in the shape of a log, filled with a delicious filling of marzipan.

Mince pies Mince pies, like many other traditional Christmas foods, contain a rich mixture of dried fruits, sugar, spices and alcohol. Nowadays, they bear little resemblance to those made in the Middle Ages when they were filled with minced meats, such as pheasant, rabbit or chicken with their livers and hearts, as well as lamb's kidneys. Mince pies were banned by the Puritans, along with other Christmas celebrations in the time of Oliver Cromwell, but came back into favour in 1660 after the Restoration. They were then round in shape rather than crib-shaped and their meat content gradually dwindled. Today, only beef suet is included with the dried fruits and crystallised peel.

Plum pudding A plum pudding, brought to the table decorated with holly and shimmering with a blue flame of burning alcohol, is a dramatic end to a Christmas meal. It is usually served with brandy butter or rum sauce, but custard and cream are also good accompaniments. Plum pudding did not become traditional at Christmas in Britain until the 19th century when it was introduced by Prince Albert who was particularly fond of it. Plum porridge was the earliest form, eaten in the Middle Ages. It was made from meat, usually beef or veal, stewed with currants, prunes, lemon juice, spices and wine, thickened with brown breadcrumbs. By the 19th century, the meat had been left out and the pudding was similar to those eaten today. The tradition of putting charms in the pudding was probably borrowed from the idea of putting a bean in the Twelfth Night cake (Gâteau Pithiviers). In the past, a coin, a thimble and a ring were put in the pudding. The ring brought a marriage, the coin brought wealth and the thimble brought a blessed life to the person who found the charm in their portion of pudding.

Yule log (Bûche de Noël) The yule log is generally associated with Christmas Eve, the last day of preparations for Christmas. In many countries, a huge log, often of cherry wood, was dragged indoors and kept alight in the hearth throughout the festive period. A yule candle was often lit at the same time on the dining table and, again, kept alight throughout Christmas to ward off evil. Cakes representing yule logs are popular in many countries, particularly in France, and often contain chocolate or chestnut purée. The traditional decoration is of marzipan holly leaves, meringue mushrooms and small figures.

Gingerbread Gingerbread has been associated with the festive season since the Middle Ages and most countries in the Christian world have their own special type, ranging from crisp biscuits to deep sponge cake. It was originally made with breadcrumbs, flavoured with ginger, aniseed, liquorice and cinnamon and moistened with red wine. Later, the breadcrumbs were replaced with flour, butter and eggs, but the mixture still contained lots of spices. In the past, children were given small gingerbread figures to represent Jesus and today gingerbread is still made into stars, candles and other festive shapes.

Shortbread This rich, buttery biscuit is traditionally served at teatime on Christmas Day or around New Year. It originates in Scotland where it was made with oatmeal; it is now made with wheat flour. Shortbread is usually baked into a large round and served cut into wedges. This shape is thought to be inherited from ancient New Year cakes which symbolised the sun. On special occasions, it can be decorated with almond slivers or pieces of crystallised orange or lemon peel. In the Shetland Islands, it is flavoured with cumin.

Fruit Fruit has always played a big part in Christmas celebrations, whether cooked in breads, pies and puddings, served in warming punches and cocktails or merely presented in a luxurious display on a sideboard or as a centrepiece. Crystallised fruits have been popular since Tudor times at special meals. They were eaten at the end of a meal, and also offered to guests at other times of day. Nowadays, they are eaten only at Christmas. An old custom in many parts of England was the wassailing of fruit trees around Christmas. A steaming wassail bowl was taken out into the orchard and people would drink the punch and throw the dregs on to the trees to encourage them to bear a rich harvest during the following year.

Poultry Poultry was eaten at the Christmas dinner table in Europe long before turkey was brought over from America early in the 16th century. Goose, chicken and pheasant were popular among ordinary people, while richer folk ate peacocks and swans. A roasted peacock would be brought to the dinner table dressed with its feathers and with a piece of brandy-soaked bread in its mouth, which was set alight just before the bird was brought into the room.

Christmas Traditions

Christmas traditions vary enormously throughout the Christian world, but many have their roots in the same legends.

Great Britain and North America Great Britain and North America share many of the customs and traditions of Christmas and most of the same traditional foods and drinks. One of the most popular traditions that is still carried out today is that of carol singing. Groups of singers visit friends' and neighbours' houses to sing them carols in the weeks leading up to Christmas. At each house they visit they are given something to eat and a warming drink, usually a mince pie and a glass of mulled wine.

Another tradition, inherited from Germany, is that of bringing indoors and decorating a Christmas tree. The whole family helps, using candles or lights, shiny ornaments and tinsel. The tree is also often decorated with cookies or chocolates, which are eaten over the festive season.

The main event is the Christmas dinner, usually turkey, Christmas pudding and mince pies. This is eaten on Christmas day at lunchtime and is usually shared with family. The dessert is usually Christmas pudding, which is made at least a month before Christmas and it is traditional for everyone in the house to help stir the pudding and to make a wish when they are doing it. Sometimes charms or coins are hidden inside the pudding and it is doused with brandy and lit just before serving.

Mistletoe is also a part of the celebrations. It has long been a symbol of friendship, especially in Britain. In the past, if friends met under mistletoe, it was a sign of good luck; and if enemies did so, it would make them stop fighting. Today it is brought indoors and anyone who stands under it will be kissed.

On Christmas Eve, as in many other parts of the world, British and American children hang stockings over the fireplace or at the ends of their beds. Often they will have written to Father Christmas beforehand to tell him what presents they would like him to leave for them when he comes to visit in the middle of the night. He is believed to come silently down the chimney during the night and fill their stockings with presents, which usually include nuts, oranges and apples as well as small gifts.

Germany In Germany, children start preparing for Christmas with an advent calender which counts down the days until Christmas Day. Nowadays, it usually has twenty-four windows, each with a picture behind, one to be opened each day until Christmas Day. In the past, it used to be twenty-four little boxes hanging on a wreath made of fir branches. Each box would contain a little gift, often something to eat. The advent calender has now also become a tradition in Britain and the United States. Also in the weeks before Christmas in some parts of Germany, children write to the Christ child, asking for presents. These they leave on the windowsill so the Christ child will see them. To make them catch his eye, they are often spread with glue and sprinkled with sugar to make them sparkle.

One traditional German story, often told on Christmas Eve, is about a woodman and his family. As they were sitting around the fire, they heard a knock on the door and were surprised to find a small boy standing outside in the snow in the forest on his own. They asked him in, and gave him something to eat and a bed for the night. The next morning, they awoke to the sound of singing. It was a choir of angels who filled the cottage with light and music. The family realised they had given shelter to the Christ child. As he left the cottage, he told them he wanted to give them something to remember him by. He touched a small fir tree nearby and it began to glow. He said it would warm their hearts and bear presents to reward them for their kindness.

Nowadays, fir trees are decorated all over the world. In Germany, it is usually the mother of the family who brings it indoors and decorates it and the children are not allowed to see it until it is finished on Christmas Eve.

Germans eat many different sorts of pastries throughout the year and some are traditionally eaten at Christmas, including gingerbread from Nuremburg, marzipan cakes from Lübeck, and the well-known stollen, particularly stollen from Dresden.

The Netherlands Saint Nicholas is the patron saint of children and in Holland, he is called Sinter Klaas, a name which has become Santa Claus in Britain and North America. Nicholas was a kind bishop who liked to help people secretly. He knew a very poor merchant who couldn't afford to give his three daughters money when they married. According to legend, one night Saint Nicholas climbed up on to the merchant's roof and dropped three small sacks of gold down the chimney for his daughters. They fell into the stockings that had been hung above the fire to dry. This is where the tradition of hanging up stockings comes from, in the hope that Saint Nicholas will fill them with presents.

Sinter Klaas parties are often held on Christmas Eve in the Netherlands. Poems are written to other members of the family, often teasing ones, and signed from Sinter Klaas. Presents are hidden around the house and more poems are written, giving clues as to where the presents are hidden. These presents are said to come from Saint Nicholas. Dutch families usually have a special cake on this evening, Letterbanket, which is made from marzipan and pastry. It is usually made in the shape of a letter, the initial of the family's name, or there are several small cakes made in the shapes of the initials of all the family members.

In Holland, the food is similar to that of northern Germany. Pastries are popular throughout the year, often flavoured with ginger, cinnamon and nutmeg. At Christmas, it is traditional to eat tiny cakes with these spices, called spéculos. Carp is another traditional dish. In some areas, carp are still fattened from summer onward to serve at Christmas. Nowadays, the Christmas meal is more likely to be goose, turkey or venison. Some foods are always eaten at Christmas in Holland, such as apples which are meant to represent the tree of knowledge, and nuts which, with their tough shells, represent life's difficulties.

Poland On Christmas Eve, Polish children watch the sky for signs of the first stars. When they appear, the Christmas feast begins. Before they start to eat, the Poles pass around a small wafer, oplatek, which is decorated with a picture of Mary, Joseph and Jesus. Each person has to break off a bit of the wafer and pass it on. In rural areas, the farm animals were also given a piece of the wafer and this privilege is still often extended to domestic pets today.

Hay or straw is spread over the floor and under the dining table during the meal to remind everyone that Jesus was born in a stable, and two empty places are left at the table in case Mary and Jesus arrive. In Poland, it is traditional to eat foods containing poppy seeds at Christmas.

Finland Christmas Eve morning in Finland is the time for people to go out and cut their Christmas tree. They bring it home on a sledge and have to decorate it in time for the party in the evening. It is also a tradition to feed birds and wild animals on Christmas Eve, to help them stay alive through the festive period. Children hang up corn sheaths and strings of nuts and suet in trees for the birds and squirrels. When the animals have been fed, everyone waits inside for Father Christmas to visit them. He comes from Lapland over the snow in a sleigh pulled by reindeer.

In the evening on Christmas Eve in Finland, the traditional meal consists of cold ham pie (made with a rye crust), salted meats, pickled herrings, turnip purée, carrots and salted cucumbers.

Norway In Norway, families start baking in early December. Many different types of biscuits and cakes are made including ulekake, a Christmas bread filled with raisins, candied peel and cardamom. The heat of all the ovens is supposed to make the first heavy winter snows melt. Norwegian children remember the Nisse, a gnome who guards farm animals. They leave a bowl of porridge out for him; if they forget, he may play tricks on them in the New Year. Traditional foods include roast pork or pork ribs served with sauerkraut flavoured with cumin. In

common with other parts of Scandinavia, the Norwegians also enjoy petits fours with cloves and ginger, fried dough fritters with brandy, and gingerbread, which is extremely popular.

Sweden In Sweden, 13 December is a special day as it is the feast of Saint Lucia. Saint Lucia was an early Christian, in the days when Christians were persecuted and had to hide in caves to pray. Saint Lucia used to take food to them, wearing a crown of candles on her head so she could find her way but had both hands free to carry food. She was caught by the Romans, but her kindness has never been forgotten. Today in Sweden, special Lucia buns and ginger snaps are eaten on her feast day. All the children get up early and the youngest girl dresses up as Saint Lucia in a long white robe and a red sash. She wears a crown of candles on her head to light the way when she carries coffee and Lucia buns to her family while they are still in bed. Other traditional Christmas foods served at the main meal on Christmas Eve are braised ham with apples, red cabbage and mustard. There is also a very old custom of marinated fish served with white sauce, potatoes, mustard and black pepper. Loaves containing crystallised fruits are also eaten over the festive period. On Christmas Day, breakfast is julhög, which consists of a ball of rye bread, a small wheat bun sprinkled with sugar, a heart-shaped piece of shortbread and a red apple served one on top of the other in a stack.

Russia A Russian legend explains why black bread was traditionally put in Christmas stockings. Baboushka was an old women who always welcomed travellers passing by her cottage. One morning, three strangers knocked at the door, dressed in rich robes. She took them in, fed them with black bread and they slept in her bed until the evening. When they left, she asked why they travelled at night. They explained that they were three kings from the East, following a star to lead them to the Christ child. She wanted to go with them, but couldn't leave her house until she had cleaned it. She followed on later with a gift of black bread. When she finally reached Bethlehem after months of travelling, only the animals were left in the stable. She left her bread in the manger so the Christ child knew she had been there. That night, she awoke to a voice telling her, "I am the Christ child. Take my hand and come with me." She closed her eyes and went to heaven that night. Apart from black bread, another traditional food eaten in Russia at Christmas is kutia, a dish of wheat grain cooked with dried fruit.

France Traditionally in France, the main celebration of Christmas is a meal on Christmas morning, taken straight after returning from midnight mass. The length of the service and the walk to and from church used to justify a large meal in the early hours of the morning. These days, throughout France, turkey and chestnuts have become the main Christmas dish but, in the past, different regions used to have different specialities. In the south-east of France, the meal would always end with the 'thirteen Christmas desserts', symbolising the thirteen diners at the Last Supper. They were pompe à l'huile (a fruit pastry), raisins, quince paste, marzipan sweets, nougat, fougasse (a rich cake), crystallised lemons, walnuts and hazelnuts, fresh pears, plums, dried figs, almonds and dates.

An ancient French custom is for godparents to give their godchildren a brioche cake, decorated with raisins and sugar in the form of a human figure such as a puppet or a baby. This is known by different names in different regions: Père Janvier in the Ardèche, cougnou in northern France.

French families often burn a log of cherry wood as a yule log. They carry it to the house on Christmas Eve and light it, sometimes after having sprinkled it with wine. It is also a custom to keep the fire alight and the candles burning, with food and drink on the table during the night in case Mary and Jesus should pass that way. Like in so many other countries, children put their shoes by the fire at night hoping to find them filled with presents in the morning.

Gâteau Pithiviers, a speciality of the Orléans region, is served on Twelfth Night. It is a pastry pie with scalloped edges stuffed with almond filling. It usually contains a bean as a charm and whoever gets the bean in their slice wears a golden crown for the day.

Italy Saint Francis of Assisi has a special place in Christmas celebrations in Italy. Hundreds of years after Jesus was born, Saint Francis went to Bethlehem to see the place where the stable had been. The next Christmas at home in Greccio in Italy, he wanted to re-enact the nativity story to remind everyone that Jesus was born in a humble stable. He built a manger in a cave with wood and straw and took in there an ox and a donkey. Village people played the parts of Mary, Joseph and the shepherds and they carved a wooden figure to represent Jesus.

Many people came to watch and one man thought he saw the eyes of Jesus open when Francis looked into the manger. After this many churches followed his idea for a Christmas crèche and the idea also spread to Italian families who have a nativity scene in their homes.

In Italy, before Christmas, children go from house to house dressed as shepherds playing pipes and singing songs. They are given money to buy Christmas food. But on Christmas Eve, Italians do without food for the whole day. After midnight mass they have a grand feast which will include panettone, the Italian Christmas cake.

Presents are not opened until Twelfth Night. This is when the three kings arrived at Bethlehem to worship Jesus. That night, children wait for the good witch, La Befana, to come down the chimney. Good children find presents in their shoes, while bad ones find pieces of coal.

Christmas is very much a family feast in Italy today and all the family are involved in the preparations for the main meal. On Christmas morning, friends and relatives drop in to exchange gifts when the preparations are taking place, and they are welcomed with sweetmeats such as nougat, nuts, biscuits and figs, prepared specially for the occasion.

Greece On Christmas Eve in Greece, young boys go out carolling in the streets. They play drums and triangles to accompany them and if they sing well, neighbours give them money, nuts, sweets and dried figs. Sometimes, they make beautiful model boats and decorate them with gold-painted nuts. These they carry proudly from house to house, a custom that still survives in many places today, particularly on the Greek Islands.

basic recipes

Fondant Moulding Paste

This icing is simple to use once you get used to its consistency and you can achieve a professional result more quickly than with royal icing. It is also easy to make, since extra sifted icing sugar can be added until it is sufficiently malleable. Use it for covering cakes: after adding a layer of marzipan to the cake, when it needs to be brushed lightly with egg white to make the icing adhere, or add it directly to a sponge or Madeira cake, after brushing the cake with apricot glaze.

It should be rolled out on a surface sprinkled with a mixture of sifted icing sugar and cornflour and, for ease of movement, it can be rolled out on a sheet of polythene sprinkled with the sugar mixture. To smooth it, simply rub using a circular motion (take care if you have long fingernails or are wearing rings) with fingertips that have been dipped in icing sugar and cornflour. The paste can be coloured by adding liquid or powder or paste food colourings; flavourings can be added, too. Apart from cake covering, it is also good for moulding all types of animals, flowers and other shapes. It can be painted with liquid food colouring for extra effect.

Fondant moulding paste can be used almost interchangeably with royal icing but take care when covering tiered cakes, since sometimes the paste does not set hard enough to take the weight of heavy top tiers. Make sure you allow plenty of time for drying out. It may help to add 1–2 coats of royal icing to the top of the cake before adding the moulding paste.

Liquid glucose or glucose syrup is available from most larger chemists and also from specialist cake decorating shops.

It is difficult to make up quantities of more than 1 kg (2 lb) of this icing because of the kneading required. It blends most easily when made in 500–750 g (1–1½ lb) quantities. Smaller quantities can be used, but the egg white and liquid glucose quantities must be weighed very accurately. If only small quantities are required, use a ready-made fondant paste, which will keep for up to a couple of months wrapped securely in clear polythene. It is obtainable in supermarkets as well as specialist cake-decorating shops.

500 g (1 lb) icing sugar
1 egg white
50 g (2 oz) liquid glucose or glucose syrup
food colouring and/or flavouring (optional)

Preparation time: 10–15 minutes

1 Sift the icing sugar into a mixing bowl to remove all lumps and make a well in the centre.

2 Add the egg white and liquid glucose. Beat with a wooden spoon or spatula, gradually pulling in the icing sugar from the sides of the bowl, to make a stiff mixture.

3 Knead the icing thoroughly, mixing in any remaining icing sugar in the bowl to give a smooth and manageable paste. To see if it is ready, press your thumb into the icing. If the indentation is perfect, the icing is ready. Add a little more icing sugar if the paste sticks to your thumb.

4 Add colouring and flavouring to the moulding paste as desired and extra sifted icing sugar, if necessary, to obtain the correct consistency – i.e. suitable for rolling, which you will soon be able to judge with practice.

5 The icing can be stored in a tightly sealed polythene bag or a plastic container in a cool place for 2–3 days.

Makes 500 g (1 lb)

Marzipan or Almond Paste

Almond paste is generally home-made and marzipan is shop-bought. Both are used for covering all cakes to be coated with royal icing and for most cakes to be covered in Fondant Moulding Paste, especially fruit cakes; for decorative tops to cakes; or for moulding all sorts of shapes, such as flowers, leaves and animals.

Make up in quantities of not more than 1 kg (2 lb) at a time, otherwise it becomes unmanageable. You can make up small quantities using 50 g (2 oz) ground almonds, etc. However, if you need small amounts for colouring, it is often best to use a commercial marzipan. The remainder, if it is securely wrapped in polythene, will keep for up to 1 month or so.

To make a creamy-white marzipan, the natural colour of almonds, use 2 lightly beaten egg whites instead of the egg or egg yolks for mixing. Marzipan cannot be stored in the freezer.

To colour marzipan, simply add several drops of the chosen food colourings, then knead and squeeze the marzipan until the colour is evenly distributed throughout, with no streaking. Powder or paste colourings can be used in the same way, adding sufficient until the required colour is obtained. If the marzipan becomes too soft, knead in a little sifted icing sugar.

Commercial marzipan is available ready to roll in the traditional yellow or white, which is in fact the natural colour. They are both good and easy to use and the natural one is ideal for colouring, as it gives truer colours than the yellow version. Make sure you buy fresh marzipan, either by checking the date on the package or by pressing it with your finger. If it is so hard that you cannot make a slight indentation, you should not buy it.

125 g (4 oz) caster sugar
125 g (4 oz) icing sugar, sifted
250 g (8 oz) ground almonds
1 teaspoon lemon juice
few drops of almond essence
1 egg or 2 egg yolks, beaten

Preparation time: about 10 minutes

1. Combine the sugars and almonds and make a well in the centre.

2. Add the lemon juice, almond essence and sufficient egg or egg yolks to mix to a firm but manageable dough.

3. Turn on to a lightly sugared surface and knead until smooth. Take care not to over-knead or the marzipan may begin to turn oily. (There is no remedy for this and it then becomes difficult to use.) It can be wrapped securely in clingfilm or aluminium foil and stored for up to 2 days before use.

Makes 500 g (1 lb)

Royal Icing

Royal icing can be made in any quantity as long as you allow 1 egg white to each 250 g (8 oz) of icing sugar. However, it is better to make up not more than a 1 kg (2 lb) quantity at a time because the icing keeps better if made in small quantities.

This icing, once made, can be stored in an airtight container in a cool place for about 2 days. However, it must be stirred very thoroughly before use, and if necessary a little extra sifted icing sugar added to correct the consistency. The icing often seems to soften if left to stand for more than a few hours.

While using the icing, cover the bowl with a damp cloth to prevent a crust forming. Egg albumen powder, available from specialist cake-decorating shops, can be made up according to the instructions on the package, and used in place of fresh egg whites. Glycerine can be added to help soften the icing. It should be used sparingly, as too much glycerine will make a very soft icing.

3 egg whites
750 g (1½ lb) icing sugar, sifted
3 teaspoons strained lemon juice
1–1½ teaspoons glycerine (optional)

Preparation time: about 15 minutes, plus standing

1. Put the egg whites into a clean, grease-free bowl and beat until frothy. Using a wooden spoon, gradually beat in half the sifted icing sugar. (A hand-held electric whisk can be used but it will incorporate a lot of air and the resulting bubbles will be difficult to disperse.)

2. Add the lemon juice, glycerine, if using, and half the remaining sugar. Beat well until smooth and very white.

3. Gradually beat in enough of the remaining icing sugar to give a consistency which will just stand in soft peaks.

4. Put the icing into an airtight container or cover the bowl with a damp cloth and leave to stand for an hour or so, if possible, to allow most of the air bubbles to come to the surface and burst.

5. The icing is now ready for coating a cake or it can be thickened a little with extra sifted icing sugar to use for piping stars, flowers and other shapes.

Makes 750 g (1½ lb)

Covering a Cake in Fondant Moulding Paste

If the cake is covered in marzipan, first brush the marzipan lightly all over with egg white. If the cake is without marzipan, brush it first with apricot glaze.

Roll out the icing either on a sheet of polythene, dredged with a mixture of icing sugar and cornflour, or directly on a work surface dredged with the same mixture. Ensure the rolling pin is also dredged with the icing sugar mixture. Roll it until it is the width of the top of the cake plus the sides, plus about 2.5 cm (1 inch) extra; this usually means about 12–15 cm (5–6 inches) larger than the top of the cake.

Support the icing on a rolling pin, pull off the polythene, if using, and place the icing centrally over the top of the cake.

Press the icing on to the sides of the cake working from the centre out to the edge, then down the sides, using your fingertips (dipped in a mixture of icing sugar and cornflour) in a circular movement to give an even covering.

Trim off the excess icing using a sharp knife. Smooth out around the base and trim again if necessary. Any wrinkles or marks can be removed by rubbing over in a circular movement with the fingers.

For square cakes, if you want straight, rather than rounded corners, cut out a piece of icing from each corner, then mould it carefully to conceal the join.

For any other shaped cake, mould the icing in the same way, but if used for a difficult shape, it will be necessary to cut the icing in one or two places to achieve a good covering. Leave for at least 24 hours to dry, and preferably 2–3 days, before adding the decoration.

Apricot Glaze

Apricot glaze can be used to help stick fondant moulding or marzipan to a cake. It can also be used to glaze the tops of cakes, covering nuts and fruits with a glossy sheen.

175 g (6 oz) apricot jam
2 tablespoons water

Preparation time: about 10 minutes
Cooking time: 5 minutes

1. Put the jam and water in a small saucepan and warm gently until the jam has melted.

2. Rub the mixture through a fine sieve and return to a clean pan.

3. Bring to a boil and simmer for 1 minute or until it reaches the required consistency. Allow to cool before use.

small
cakes & bakes

orange gingerbread

This moist cake flavoured with ginger and corn syrup was believed to have been introduced to Europe during the time of the crusades. At Pithiviers in France, however, it is held that gingerbread was introduced by St Gregory, an Armenian bishop who took refuge there in the 11th century. Whatever the case, it was from that time on that the manufacture of gingerbread spread into Holland, England, Germany, Belgium, France and Italy. Gingerbread was formerly regarded as a fairground delicacy and in Paris the Gingerbread Fair had been held at an abbey since the 11th century. The monks sold their own gingerbread cakes there in different shapes at Christmas.

Preparation time: 30 minutes
Cooking time: 1½–1¾ hours

500 g (1 lb) plain flour
1 tablespoon ground ginger
3 teaspoons baking powder
1 teaspoon bicarbonate of soda
pinch of salt
175 g (6 oz) butter or margarine
4 tablespoons dark golden syrup
500 g (1 lb) dark brown sugar
150 ml (¼ pint) milk
2 eggs
finely grated rind and juice of
  1 large orange
16 slices of crystallised or
  preserved ginger, to decorate

1   Heat the oven to 160°C (325°F), Gas Mark 3.

2   Sift the flour, ginger, baking powder, soda and salt into a large mixing bowl.

3   Put the butter or margarine and the syrup into a saucepan, stir over a low heat until the butter has melted, then add the sugar, and continue stirring until the sugar has completely melted. Do not overheat. Add the melted ingredients to the flour mixture and beat well. Warm the milk in the saucepan in which the ingredients were melted, stirring well to absorb any sugar mixture that might have been left in the pan. Pour this over the ingredients in the mixing bowl and stir briskly. Lastly add the eggs, orange juice and rind, and beat well. The mixture will appear very soft, but that is quite correct.

4   Line a 20 cm (8 inch) square cake tin with greaseproof paper and grease this very well. Pour in the mixture. Bake in the oven for 1½–1¾ hours, then cool in the tin. Cut into 16 squares. Top each square with a slice of ginger.

Makes 16 squares

variation: moist orange cake

a   Use the grated rind and juice of the orange as in the recipe above, but substitute 150 ml (¼ pint) orange juice for the milk. Do not use the dark brown sugar but use light brown sugar instead which gives the cake a lovely colour. Top each square with a crystallised orange slice.

b   Bake the basic recipe or the variation above in a 23 cm (9 inch) cake tin to produce about twenty-five shallow squares of cake. Bake the cake for 1 hour 20 minutes at the temperature above.

sally lunns

These traditional English teacakes are named after an 18th-century baker whose store can still be visited in the town of Bath. Sally Lunns can also be served cold topped with glacé icing.

Preparation time: 45 minutes
Cooking time: 20–25 minutes

500 g (1 lb) plain flour
1 teaspoon salt
25 g (1 oz) fresh yeast
1 teaspoon sugar
2 eggs
1 egg yolk
250 ml (8 fl oz) single cream
4 tablespoons lukewarm water

Glaze:
4 tablespoons milk
3 teaspoons caster sugar

1 Heat the oven to 200°C (400°F), Gas Mark 6.

2 Place the flour and salt in a large bowl. In a separate bowl, cream the yeast with the sugar. Beat the whole eggs and egg yolk and strain into the creamed yeast mixture. Stir in the cream and whisk until frothy. Add the lukewarm water. Pour the yeast mixture into the flour and mix to a soft dough, adding a little more water if necessary. Beat well, then cover with lightly oiled clingfilm and a clean kitchen towel. Put in a warm place to rise for about 1½ hours or until doubled in size.

3 Turn the dough on to a lightly floured work surface and knead lightly. Halve the dough and shape into two rounds about 20 cm (8 inches) in diameter. Put the rounds into two greased 20 cm (8 inch) cake tins. Bake in the oven for 20–25 minutes.

4 Combine the milk and sugar and heat gently to dissolve the sugar. Remove the cakes from the oven, brush with the glaze, and return to the oven for 30 seconds to dry the glaze. Serve warm with butter, or slice the cake, toast it and spread with butter.

Makes 2

puff pastry mince pies

In Britain mince pies are traditionally served throughout the whole of the Christmas period, usually with a cup of tea or coffee. They can be eaten warm or cold with or without cream. Some people like to serve mince pies with a piece of Stilton cheese.

Preparation time: 20–25 minutes
Cooking time: 25 minutes

500 g (1 lb) puff pastry
1 egg, beaten, for brushing
250 g (8 oz) mincemeat
3 tablespoons flaked almonds
double cream, to serve (optional)

1 Heat the oven to 200°C (400°F), Gas Mark 6.

2 Roll out the pastry quite thinly and use a glass or biscuit cutter to cut out twelve rounds, 7 cm (3 inches) in diameter, and twelve rounds, 5 cm (2 inches) in diameter.

3 Line twelve patty tins with the larger pastry rounds and brush the edges with beaten egg. Put a teaspoonful of mincemeat into each pastry case. Lay a smaller pastry round over the top of the mincemeat and press down gently with the rim of an egg-cup – this helps to seal the two pastry surfaces together.

4 Brush the top of each pie with beaten egg and sprinkle with flaked almonds. Bake in the oven for 25 minutes or until puffed and golden.

5 Serve warm, with double cream, if liked.

Makes 12

old-fashioned penny buns

These buns originated in Britain.

Preparation time: 40 minutes, plus rising
Cooking time: 15–20 minutes

625 g (1½ lb) plain flour
½ teaspoon salt
15 g (½ oz) fresh yeast
50 g (2 oz), plus ½ teaspoon sugar
575 ml (18 fl oz) lukewarm milk
90 g (3 oz) butter
1 egg, beaten
90 g (3 oz) currants

Glaze:
50 g (2 oz) sugar
125 ml (4 fl oz) water

1 Heat the oven to 200°C (400°F), Gas Mark 6.

2 Place 300 g (10 oz) flour and the salt in a large bowl. Cream the yeast with ½ teaspoon sugar in a small bowl. Stir in about 125 ml (4 fl oz) milk until dissolved.

3 Make a well in the flour and pour in the yeast mixture. Mix to a soft dough, using a little more milk if necessary, and beat well. Cover with lightly oiled clingfilm and set aside to rise for 30–40 minutes.

4 Warm the remaining milk and melt the butter in it. Allow to cool to lukewarm, then add the egg. Stir into the risen flour mixture together with the currants, the remaining flour and sugar. Beat well, then cover the bowl with lightly oiled clingfilm and a clean kitchen towel. Set aside to rise in a warm place for about 1½ hours or until doubled in size.

5 Turn on to a floured work surface, punch your fist into the dough, and knead lightly. Shape pieces of the dough into small buns and place on a greased baking sheet so the buns are just touching each other. Cover loosely with a cloth and allow to rise for 15 minutes.

6 Bake the buns for 15–20 minutes. Meanwhile, make the glaze. Put the sugar and water in a small saucepan and heat gently, stirring until the sugar dissolves. Increase the heat and boil for 3 minutes, without stirring.

7 Remove the buns from the oven, brush with the glaze, and return to the oven for about 30 seconds to dry the glaze. Serve warm from the oven, with or without butter.

Makes 15

greek baklava

Preparation time: 25 minutes
Cooking time: 25 minutes

75 g (3 oz) blanched almonds,
   finely chopped
75 g (3 oz) walnuts, finely chopped
½ teaspoon ground cinnamon
½ teaspoon ground mixed spice
150 ml (¼ pint) clear honey
400 g (13 oz) packet frozen puff
   pastry, defrosted
20 g (¾ oz) butter, melted
2 tablespoons lemon juice

1 Heat the oven to 200°C (400°F), Gas Mark 6.

2 Mix the almonds with the walnuts, cinnamon, mixed spice and 2 tablespoons of the honey. Roll out the dough into a 33 cm (13 inch) square. Cut into four squares. Place one square in a 41 cm (16½ inch) shallow, square cake tin lined with aluminium foil. Brush with a little butter. Cover with another square then spread the nut filling over it. Cover with the third square, brush again with butter, then cover with the remaining square. Brush with butter and cut through the top two layers to mark out four squares. Cut each in half again to make triangles. Bake for 25 minutes.

3 Meanwhile, mix the lemon juice with the remaining honey and make up to 150 ml (¼ pint) with water. Bring to the boil and simmer for 2 minutes. Spoon over the hot baklava still in its tin and leave to soak for 2 hours before removing from the tin to serve.

Makes 8

greek halva

Preparation time: 5 minutes, plus chilling
Cooking time: 20–25 minutes

1 Heat the oil in a large shallow frying pan over gentle heat. Pour in the semolina in a fine, steady stream, stirring continuously. Cook gently, stirring from time to time, until all the oil has been absorbed and the semolina is pale golden.

2 Stir in the sugar, milk and wine. Cook for 10 minutes, stirring continuously, until the mixture is thick and will hold its shape on a wooden spoon (take care that it does not burn.) Pour into a lightly greased shallow rectangular dish or tin 20 x 30 cm (8 x 12 inches) or use two smaller tins if preferred, and level off the surface with a spatula. Chill for about 4 hours until firm.

3 To serve, dust lightly with cinnamon, cut into squares or rectangles, and serve with strong black coffee. Can be stored, chilled, for up to 3 days.

Makes about 36 pieces

250 ml (8 fl oz) olive oil
750 g (1½ lb) fine semolina
500 g (1 lb) sugar
750 ml (1¼ pints) milk
250 ml (8 fl oz) dry Greek white
   wine
ground cinnamon, for dusting

marron meringues

These French chestnut meringues will keep for up to 10 days if stored in an airtight container, but once assembled chill, and serve within 2–3 hours.

Preparation time: about 30 minutes
Cooking time: 2–2¼ hours

75 g (3 oz) light soft brown sugar
75 g (3 oz) caster sugar
3 egg whites

Filling:
265 g (8½ oz) sweetened chestnut
    purée
1 tablespoon rum or coffee liqueur
150 ml (¼ pint) double cream

1 Heat the oven to 110°C (225°F), Gas Mark ¼.

2 Cover two baking sheets with nonstick baking paper or greased greaseproof paper.

3 Sift the brown sugar and caster sugar together until evenly blended.

4 Put the egg whites into a clean grease-free bowl and whisk until very stiff and standing in peaks. Whisk in the sugar mixture, 1 tablespoon at a time, until it is thoroughly incorporated and the meringue is stiff again, before adding more sugar. The last third of the sugar can be whisked in or folded in as preferred. Put the meringue into a piping bag fitted with a large star nozzle and pipe into 10 cm (4 inch) bars.

5 Bake in the oven for 2 hours, reversing the baking sheets in the oven after 1 hour. The meringues should then be set and peel easily off the paper; if not, cook for a further 15 minutes and try again. Leave to cool on the paper on a wire rack.

6 When they are cold, peel the meringues from the paper and store in an airtight container until required.

7 To assemble, combine the chestnut spread and rum or liqueur and beat until quite smooth. Whip the cream until stiff and fold through the chestnut mixture. Sandwich the meringues together with the chestnut cream. Chill until required.

Makes 12

honey cakes

Preparation time: 40 minutes, plus chilling and cooling
Cooking time: 30–35 minutes

500 g (1 lb) clear honey
6 tablespoons water
500 g (1 lb) black treacle
700 g (1½ lb) wholemeal flour
300 g (10 oz) rye flour
1 tablespoon baking powder
1 teaspoon bicarbonate of soda
1 tablespoon milk

Filling:
125 g (4 oz) almond paste
140 g (4½ oz) caster sugar
1 egg white
1 tablespoon rum
10 glacé cherries, chopped
10 pieces of angelica, chopped
125 g (4 oz) blanched almonds,
  chopped
milk, for brushing

To finish:
325 g (11 oz) plain chocolate,
  broken into pieces
glacé cherries and angelica, to
  decorate

1   Melt the honey and gradually bring to the boil with the water and black treacle. Leave to cool.

2   Work in the flours and the baking powder. Dissolve the bicarbonate of soda in the milk and stir into the mixture. Wrap in aluminium foil and leave for 2 days at room temperature.

3   To make the filling, break the almond paste into small pieces and mix with the sugar, egg white, rum, cherries, angelica, and almonds. Stand over a saucepan of hot water and mix well.

4   Heat the oven to 190°C (375°F), Gas Mark 5. Grease three baking sheets. Divide the cake mixture into three pieces.

5   Roll each piece out to a 1.5 cm (¾ inch) thickness and cut out two heart shapes from each portion. Spread the filling over the centre of half the hearts, brush the edges with milk, top with a second heart, and press the edges well together.

6   Bake the cakes for 30–35 minutes then leave to cool. Melt the chocolate in a bowl over hot water, ice the cakes all over, and top with glacé cherries and pieces of angelica.

Makes 30

austrian jam rings

Preparation time: 40 minutes, plus chilling and cooling
Cooking time: 10 minutes

400 g (14 oz) plain flour
200 g (7 oz) butter, cut into flakes
3 egg yolks
125 g (4 oz) caster sugar
25 g (1 oz) vanilla sugar
grated rind and juice of 1 lemon
50 g (2 oz) ground hazelnuts or
    pecans
125 g (4 oz) strawberry jam
icing sugar, for sprinkling

1 Sift the flour into a mixing bowl and add the butter. Put the egg yolks, sugar, vanilla sugar, lemon rind and nuts in the centre, and knead all the ingredients to a pastry dough. Wrap in aluminium foil or clingfilm and leave in the refrigerator for 2 hours.

2 Heat the oven to 200°C (400°F), Gas Mark 6. Roll out the dough on a floured surface to a thickness of about 5 mm (¼ inch) and cut into an equal number of 6 cm (2½ inch) circles and rings. Place on a greased baking sheet and bake for 10 minutes, until golden brown.

3 Carefully lift the circles and rings from the baking sheet with a palette knife and leave to cool on a wire rack.

4 Mix the jam with the lemon juice. Sift icing sugar generously over the ring biscuits. Spread the round biscuits with the jam and put a ring biscuit on the top of each one.

Makes 24

french madeleines

Preparation time: 30 minutes, plus chilling
Cooking time: 10–15 minutes

1 For the madeleines you will need the traditional small shell-shaped tins. Grease the tins with butter. (If you have no madeleine tins, use individual patty or brioche tins.)

2 Mix the sugar and sifted flour together in a bowl. Melt but do not brown the butter. Mix the eggs into the flour and sugar mixture with a wooden spoon and gradually add the cooled butter, salt, ground almonds, orange flower water and vanilla essence. Cover and leave for 1 hour in the refrigerator.

3 Heat the oven to 200°C (400°F), Gas Mark 6. Half-fill the greased tins with the cake mixture and bake for 10–15 minutes. Carefully remove from the tins and leave to cool on a wire rack

Makes 20

125 g (4 oz) caster sugar
125 g (4 oz) self-raising flour, sifted
125 g (4 oz) butter
3 eggs, beaten
pinch of salt
50 g (2 oz) ground almonds
2 teaspoons orange flower water
¼ teaspoon vanilla essence

ravanie

These diamond-shaped orange cakes are from Greece.

Preparation time: 30–40 minutes
Cooking time: 1¼ hours

125 g (4 oz) butter, softened
250 g (8 oz) caster sugar
175 g (6 oz) plain flour
2 teaspoons baking powder
pinch of salt
½ teaspoon mixed spice
50 g (2 oz) fine semolina
finely grated rind and juice of
    2 oranges
2 eggs
1 tablespoon sesame seeds

Syrup glaze:
125 g (4 oz) sugar
finely grated rind and juice of
    1 orange
2 tablespoons clear honey

To decorate:
2 tablespoons sesame seeds,
    lightly toasted

1 Heat the oven to 180°C (350°F), Gas Mark 4. Grease a 25 x 18 cm (10 x 7 inch) rectangular tin and line with greaseproof paper or nonstick baking paper.

2 Cream the butter and sugar until pale and fluffy; this can be done by hand, with an electric mixer or in a food processor. Sift together the flour, baking powder, salt and mixed spice. Add to the creamed mixture, together with the semolina, orange rind and juice, eggs and sesame seeds. Mix well until blended.

3 Spread the mixture evenly in the prepared tin and bake in the oven for about 1¼ hours, until firm but spongy to the touch.

4 Meanwhile, make the syrup glaze. Put the sugar, orange rind, and juice into a saucepan and stir over a gentle heat until the sugar has dissolved. Add the honey and boil gently for 3 minutes.

5 When the cake is ready, remove it from the oven and pierce it at evenly spaced intervals with a fine skewer. Spoon the syrup glaze evenly over the top. Sprinkle with the toasted sesame seeds. Leave to cool.

6 Cut into diamond shapes and serve. This cake keeps for up to 1 week, covered with aluminium foil, in a cool place.

Serves 8–10

swiss honey bars

Preparation time: 30 minutes, plus standing and cooling
Cooking time: 45–50 minutes

375 g (12 oz) thick honey
375 g (12 oz) sugar
100 g (3½ oz) blanched almonds
100 g (3½ oz) hazelnuts or pecans
100 g (3½ oz) walnuts
250 g (8 oz) chopped mixed peel
grated rind of 1 lemon
625 g (1¼ lb) plain flour, sifted
1 teaspoon ground cinnamon
2 teaspoons ground cloves
generous pinch of grated nutmeg
½ teaspoon bicarbonate of soda
2 tablespoons arrack or ouzo
   (aniseed liqueur)
2 tablespoons cherry brandy

1 Bring the honey to the boil with 250 g (8 oz) of the sugar, stirring
   continuously.

2 Finely chop the almonds, hazelnuts or pecans and walnuts. Combine the
   nuts with the mixed peel, lemon rind and sifted flour. Stir in the cinnamon,
   cloves, nutmeg and bicarbonate of soda, and mix well with the hot honey
   mixture. Knead in the arrack or ouzo and cherry brandy, form into a ball,
   cover and leave to stand at room temperature for 1 day.

3 Heat the oven to 180°C (350°F), Gas Mark 4. Grease a baking sheet and roll
   out the dough to 1 cm (½ inch) thick. Place on the baking sheet and bake for
   30–35 minutes in the centre of the oven.

4 Bring the remaining sugar to the boil with a little water. Spread quickly
   over the cake while still warm and cut into bars on the baking sheet. Leave
   to cool.

Makes 20

dutch zebras

These Dutch biscuits are named 'zebras' due to their black and white striped appearance.

Preparation time: 30 minutes, plus chilling
Cooking time: 15–20 minutes

250 g (8 oz) butter
200 g (7 oz) caster sugar
½ teaspoon salt
4 egg yolks
250 g (8 oz) plain flour
100 g (3½ oz) cornflour
½ teaspoon baking powder
2 tablespoons rum
4 tablespoons cocoa powder
2 tablespoons sugar crystals

1 Cream the butter with the sugar and salt until light and fluffy. Add the egg yolks one at a time and beat well until smooth. Sift the flour with the cornflour and baking powder, add to the butter mixture, and knead to a firm dough. Halve the dough; mix the rum into one half and the sifted cocoa powder into the other. Cover both portions and leave for 1 hour in the refrigerator.

2 Heat the oven to 190°C (375°F), Gas Mark 5. Roll out the light and dark dough separately on a floured board until very thin (about 1 mm/⅟₁₆ inch). Halve each portion and place the pieces of light and dark dough alternately one upon the other, to make four striped layers. Press together well and cut into small strips. Sprinkle each strip with the sugar crystals and press the sugar in slightly.

3 Place on greased baking sheets and bake for 15–20 minutes.

4 Remove the biscuits from the baking sheets with a palette knife and leave to cool on a wire rack.

Makes 30

filhos de natal

These knot-shaped Christmas fritters from Portugal are traditionally served dipped in honey. Here they are sprinkled with caster sugar. Filhos de natal are best eaten fresh and are delicious served with coffee.

Preparation time: 40 minutes, plus rising
Cooking time: about 30 minutes

2 teaspoons dried yeast

1 teaspoon caster sugar

3 tablespoons lukewarm milk

550 g (1 lb 2 oz) strong white flour

1 teaspoon salt

4 eggs, beaten

3 tablespoons brandy

oil, for deep-frying

approx 4 tablespoons caster sugar,
  for sprinkling

1 Dissolve the yeast and sugar in the milk and leave to stand in a warm place until frothy – about 20 minutes.

2 Sift the flour and salt into a bowl and make a well in the centre. Pour in the yeast liquid, beaten eggs and brandy and mix to a smooth, elastic dough. Knead on a floured surface for 5 minutes by hand or for 2–3 minutes in a large electric mixer fitted with a dough hook. Replace the dough in the bowl, cover with greased clingfilm or a damp cloth and leave to rise in a warm place for about 2 hours, or until doubled in size.

3 Knock back the dough and knead until smooth. Roll out on a floured surface to about 5 mm (¼ inch) thick. Cut the dough into strips about 7–10 cm (3–4 inches) long and 1 cm (½ inch) wide and tie loosely into knots.

4 Heat the oil to about 190°C (375°F) or until a cube of bread browns in 30 seconds, and fry the fritters a few at a time until golden brown, turning over when necessary. Remove with a slotted spoon and drain on kitchen paper.

5 Sprinkle the fritters with caster sugar. Serve warm.

Makes about 40

lemon bars

If you do not have the right shape of biscuit cutter, make a cardboard pattern and use it to help you cut out the arcs.

Preparation time: 20 minutes, plus chilling
Cooking time: 10–15 minutes

150 g (5 oz) butter
125 g (4 oz) caster sugar
1 egg
grated rind of 1 lemon
generous pinch each of ground
  cinnamon, ground cloves and
  grated nutmeg
125 g (4 oz) plain flour
125 g (4 oz) hazelnuts or pecans,
  finely chopped
125 g (4 oz) fresh white
  breadcrumbs
1 egg yolk, beaten, for glazing
50 g (2 oz) blanched almonds

1 Beat the butter with the sugar, egg, lemon rind and spices. Mix the sifted flour with the nuts and breadcrumbs, add to the butter mixture, and knead all the ingredients quickly to a dough. Cover and leave for 2 hours in the refrigerator.

2 Heat the oven to 200°C (400°F), Gas Mark 6. Roll out the dough to 5 mm (¼ inch) thick. Cut out small scalloped arcs 6 cm (2½ inches) long and 2.5 cm (1 inch) wide. Place on greased baking sheets and brush with beaten egg yolk. Place a blanched almond on each biscuit and bake for 10–15 minutes.

Makes 25

cinnamon balls

Preparation time: 15 minutes
Cooking time: 25–30 minutes

1 Beat the butter or margarine with the sugar until light and creamy. Beat in the lemon rind and salt and the eggs, one at a time. Sift the flour with the baking powder and fold into the mixture with a metal spoon.

2 In a deep-fryer, heat the oil to 180°C (350°F). Using two floured teaspoons, form the dough into small balls; fry about eight balls at a time in the hot oil until golden. This will take about 5–6 minutes; turn halfway through cooking.

3 Remove the balls with a draining spoon and drain on kitchen paper. Mix the sugar with the cinnamon and sprinkle over the balls while still warm.

Makes 40

75 g (3 oz) butter or margarine
75 g (3 oz) caster sugar
grated rind of ½ lemon
pinch of salt
4 eggs
425 g (14 oz) plain flour
1 teaspoon baking powder
125 g (4 oz) sugar, for sprinkling
2 teaspoons ground cinnamon
oil, for deep-frying

honeycake hearts

In ancient times, honey was regarded as the food of the gods, a symbol of wealth and happiness used both as a food and as an offering.

Preparation time: 30 minutes
Cooking time: 20 minutes

140 g (4½ oz) caster sugar
40 g (1½ oz) butter
250 g (8 oz) honey
1 large egg
pinch of salt
25 g (1 oz) chopped mixed peel
½ teaspoon ground cinnamon
½ teaspoon ground cloves
500 g (1 lb) plain flour
1 teaspoon baking powder

Filling and icing:
125 g (4 oz) redcurrant jelly
125 g (4 oz) plain chocolate, broken
  into pieces

1 Grease one or two baking sheets with butter or margarine. Heat the oven to 220°C (425°F), Gas Mark 7.

2 Heat the sugar and butter with the honey, stirring continuously until all the ingredients have melted to give a smooth mixture. Remove from the heat and stir frequently until lukewarm. Beat the egg with the salt. Add the mixed peel to the honey mixture with the beaten egg, cinnamon, cloves and the flour sifted with the baking powder.

3 Knead well and roll out to about 3 cm (1¼ inches) thick on a floured pastry board. Cut out small heart shapes, place on the baking sheets, and bake for 8–10 minutes in the centre of the oven.

4 While still warm, sandwich the hearts together with redcurrant jelly.

5 Melt the chocolate in a bowl over a saucepan of hot water and dip one half of the cooled biscuits into the chocolate.

Makes 25

variation: Do not sandwich pairs of biscuits together, simply coat one side of each one with melted chocolate and sprinkle with chopped pistachios.

almond petits fours

The French name 'petits fours' is used to describe a variety of small cakes and biscuits, often highly decorated, which are served with coffee, usually after a dessert. They must be very small and elegant, just the size of one mouthful. The term 'petits fours' which translates as 'little oven' is thought to date back to the 18th century and originated because these cakes were cooked in a slower brick oven once the larger cakes had been removed and the temperature of the oven had dropped.

Preparation time: 15 minutes
Cooking time: 20–25 minutes

125 g (4 oz) ground almonds
125 g (4 oz) caster sugar
few drops of almond essence
2 egg whites, whisked until stiff
glacé cherries or flaked almonds,
  to decorate

1 Heat the oven to 150°C (300°F), Gas Mark 2.

2 Stir the ground almonds, caster sugar and almond essence into the egg whites. Line a baking sheet with nonstick baking or greased greaseproof paper. Place the mixture in a piping bag with a large star nozzle and pipe the mixture into circles. Put a piece of glacé cherry, or flaked almonds if preferred, on to each of the petits fours.

3 Bake in the oven for 20–25 minutes. Cool on a wire rack.

Makes about 24

almond spice bars

Preparation time: 20 minutes, plus chilling
Cooking time: 20 minutes

4 eggs
250 g (8 oz) caster sugar
425 g (14 oz) plain flour
½ teaspoon baking powder
425 g (14 oz) ground almonds
100 g (4 oz) chopped mixed peel
1 teaspoon ground cinnamon
generous pinch each of ground
  cloves, nutmeg and allspice
1 egg yolk, beaten
blanched almonds, halved

1 Beat the eggs with the sugar until pale and creamy. Sift the flour with the baking powder and mix with the ground almonds, chopped peel and spices. Stir all these ingredients into the egg mixture to form a dough. Wrap in aluminium foil or clingfilm and leave for 2 hours in the refrigerator.

2 Heat the oven to 180°C (350°F), Gas Mark 4.

3 Roll out the dough on a floured board to about 5 mm (¼ inch) thick and cut into equal-sized bars. Place on greased baking sheets. Thin the beaten egg yolk with a little water and use it to brush the bars. Place an almond half in each corner and bake for 20 minutes, until golden. Remove from the baking sheets with a palette knife and leave to cool on a wire rack.

Makes 20

baking tray honey cake

Preparation time: 20 minutes, plus chilling
Cooking time: 30 minutes

500 g (1 lb) clear or thick honey
125 ml (4 fl oz) oil
250 g (8 oz) caster sugar
750 g (1½ lb) plain flour
1 tablespoon baking powder
250 g (8 oz) ground almonds
2 teaspoons ground cinnamon
½ teaspoon ground allspice
pinch of ground cloves
pinch of salt
3 eggs
200 g (7 oz) chopped mixed peel
2 tablespoons evaporated milk

To decorate:
almond halves
glacé cherries
candied lemon peel

1 Bring the honey to the boil with the oil and sugar, stirring continuously. Allow to cool. Sift the flour with the baking powder and mix with the ground almonds, spices, salt, eggs and mixed peel. Add the honey mixture and knead well. If the dough is too soft, add a little more flour. Cover and leave for 1 hour in the refrigerator.

2 Heat the oven to 190°C (375°F), Gas Mark 5 and grease two 33 x 23 cm (13 x 9 inch) Swiss roll tins. With floured hands, press the mixture into the prepared tins, smooth the surface, and brush with the evaporated milk. Lightly cut 7 cm (3 inch) squares in the mixture with a sharp knife.

3 Decorate each square with almonds, cherries and pieces of candied lemon peel. Bake in the centre of the oven for 25–30 minutes.

4 Leave to cool slightly then remove from the baking sheet, and divide into squares.

Serves 24

marshmallow crescents

Preparation time: 30 minutes, plus chilling
Cooking time: 20 minutes

1 Beat the marshmallows with the softened butter until pale and creamy. Add the egg, vanilla sugar and salt, and mix well. Sift the flour with the baking powder and gradually stir into the marshmallow mixture. Form into a ball, wrap in aluminium foil and chill in the refrigerator until firm, about 20 minutes.

2 Heat the oven to 180°C (350°F), Gas Mark 4. Quarter the dough and roll each piece into a long thin strip. Cut into 10 cm (4 inch) lengths, form into small crescents. Bake on a baking sheet for 10–15 minutes, until golden.

3 Carefully remove from the baking sheet with a palette knife and leave to cool on a wire rack. Melt the chocolate by standing it in a bowl over hot water then dip the tips of the crescents into the chocolate. Allow the chocolate to dry thoroughly before storing the biscuits in an airtight container.

Makes 25

175 g (6 oz) white marshmallows
100 g (3½ oz) butter, softened
1 egg
1 tablespoon vanilla sugar
generous pinch of salt
300 g (10 oz) plain flour
½ teaspoon baking powder
50 g (2 oz) plain chocolate, broken
  into pieces

chocolate rum truffles

Chocolate truffles, which keep for only a short time, are traditionally given at Christmas in France and make a lovely gift if boxed. They are a good accompaniment to coffee and earn their name from the similarity to the real truffle 'fresh from the earth'! For an elegant touch, serve these delicious, rich truffles in paper bonbon cups.

Preparation time: 30 minutes, plus cooling and chilling
Cooking time: 10 minutes

75 g (3 oz) plain chocolate, broken
  into pieces
25 g (1 oz) unsalted butter
125 g (4 oz) icing sugar, sifted
2 tablespoons dark rum
cocoa powder

1 Melt the chocolate in a bowl over a saucepan of simmering water. Remove from the heat and let cool.

2 Beat the butter and icing sugar together until light and fluffy. Add the cooled, melted chocolate and rum and stir until thoroughly combined. Cover and refrigerate the mixture until firm.

3 Remove the chocolate mixture from the refrigerator and shape the mixture into 2.5 cm (1 inch) balls. Roll each ball in the cocoa powder and place on a wax paper-lined baking sheet. Refrigerate the truffles until firm. Remove the truffles from the refrigerator and let stand at room temperature for 30 minutes before serving.

Makes about 16

dutch raisin doughnuts

These small cakes, made of deep-fried yeast dough, are traditionally dusted with spiced sugar or iced and are often made in ring-shapes. Doughnuts are often served on New Year's Eve.

Preparation time: 30 minutes, plus standing
Cooking time: 40 minutes

500 g (1 lb) plain flour

40 g (1½ oz) fresh yeast

100 g (3½ oz) caster sugar

6 tablespoons lukewarm milk

pinch of salt

grated rind of 1 lemon

grated rind of 1 orange

2 eggs

75 g (3 oz) butter, cut into flakes

100 g (3½ oz) raisins

50 g (2 oz) currants

75 g (3 oz) candied orange peel,
  finely chopped

oil, for deep-frying

1 Sift the flour into a bowl and make a well in the centre. Cream the yeast with a little of the sugar and half the milk and pour into the well. Sprinkle with a little of the flour, cover, and leave to stand in a warm place for 15 minutes.

2 Mix the rest of the sugar with the remaining milk, the salt, lemon and orange rind, eggs and flaked butter, and beat into the flour. Mix all the ingredients to a stiff dough. Knead for a few minutes then leave to stand in a warm place for 15 minutes.

3 Simmer the raisins and currants for 2 minutes in hot water, drain, and mix into the dough with the candied orange peel. Leave the dough to stand for a further 30 minutes.

4 Heat the oil for frying to 190°C (375°F). Using two floured tablespoons, cut the dough into small doughnuts and fry six at a time in the oil for about 10 minutes, until golden brown. Halfway through the frying time, turn the doughnuts with a skimmer or spatula.

5 Lift out the cooked doughnuts with the draining spoon and drain on kitchen paper.

Makes 25

rhine rum fritters

Preparation time: 20 minutes
Cooking time: 20 minutes

75 g (3 oz) butter or margarine
50 g (2 oz) caster sugar
1 egg
2 tablespoons rum
250 g (8 oz) plain flour
3 tablespoons milk
pinch of salt
icing sugar, for sprinkling
oil, for deep-frying

1 Melt the butter or margarine, remove from the heat and beat with the sugar, egg and rum until frothy. Sift the flour into a bowl, make a well in the centre and add the milk, salt and the butter mixture. Knead to a workable dough.

2 Heat the oil to 190°C (375°F) in a deep frying pan. Roll out the dough on a floured board to 3 mm (⅛ inch) thick. Using a pastry wheel, cut out diamond shapes. Add six fritters at a time to the hot oil and fry for 4–5 minutes until golden; turn halfway through cooking with a draining spoon.

3 Lift out the cooked fritters and drain on kitchen paper. Sift icing sugar over them while still warm.

Makes 15

brandy fritters

Preparation time: 30 minutes
Cooking time: 20 minutes

1 Sift the flour with the baking powder into a bowl. Dot over the butter or margarine. Add the sugar, salt, eggs, milk and grappa, and knead all the ingredients to a smooth dough.

2 Heat the oil for frying to 180°C (350°F). Roll out the dough on a floured board to 3 mm (⅛ inch) thick and cut into 3.5 cm (1½ inch) squares. Add 5 fritters at a time to the hot oil and fry for 4–6 minutes until golden; turn halfway through cooking with a draining spoon.

3 Lift out the fritters when cooked and drain on kitchen paper. Sift icing sugar over them while still warm.

Makes 15

425 g (14 oz) plain flour
½ teaspoon baking powder
25 g (1 oz) butter or margarine, cut into flakes
50 g (2 oz) caster sugar
pinch of salt
2 eggs, beaten
6 tablespoons milk
1 tablespoon grappa (Italian brandy)
icing sugar, for sprinkling
oil, for deep-frying

biscuits & cookies

cinnamon shortbread

The mixture can be pressed into a decorative shortbread mould, if you have one. Traditionally these moulds were made of carved wood. Dust the shortbread liberally with caster sugar to make unmoulding the mixture on to the baking sheet easier.

Preparation time: 15 minutes, plus chilling
Cooking time: 40 minutes

150 g (5 oz) plain flour
pinch of salt
1 teaspoon ground cinnamon
25 g (1 oz) ground rice
50 g (2 oz) caster sugar
125 g (4 oz) butter
caster sugar, for dusting

1 Sift the flour, salt, cinnamon and ground rice into a bowl and stir in the sugar. Rub in the butter then knead until smooth but not sticky. Wrap in clingfilm and chill for 30 minutes.

2 Press the dough out to an 18 cm (7 inch) round and place on a greased baking sheet. Flute the edge and prick all over with a fork. Mark into eight portions and chill for 30 minutes.

3 Heat the oven to 160°C (325°F), Gas Mark 3.

4 Bake for about 40 minutes or until pale golden. Leave on the baking sheet for 10 minutes, then transfer to a wire rack to cool. Dust with sugar to serve.

Serves 8

butter shortbread

Shortbread makes a delightful gift at Christmas. For a traditional Scottish feel place in a decorative box and tie up with tartan ribbon.

Preparation time: 15–20 minutes
Cooking time: 30–35 minutes

125 g (4 oz) plain flour
50 g (2 oz) cornflour
50 g (2 oz) caster sugar
125 g (4 oz) butter

1   Heat the oven to 160°C (325°F), Gas Mark 3.

2   Sift together the flour and cornflour. Add the sugar and rub in the butter. The mixture will become crumbly at first but continue rubbing in with your fingers until it clings together in heavy lumps.

3   Turn on to a board or working surface lightly dusted with flour or cornflour and knead lightly. Roll out to a 20 cm (8 inch) circle and place on a greased baking sheet. Prick all over the top with a fork, mark into eight or ten portions, and flute the edges with your fingers.

4   Bake for 30–35 minutes until the shortbread is cooked but not browned. Leave on the baking sheet for 10 minutes, then lift off with a fish slice and place carefully on a wire rack to cool.

Serves 8–10

traditional shortbread

Shortbread is a biscuit which is rich in butter and usually served with tea. It originates from Scotland and is traditionally eaten during Christmas and the New Year. For special occasions it is decorated with candied lemon or orange peel and slivered almonds. Shortbread is usually baked in a large round and served cut from the centre into triangles; it is a relic of the ancient New Year cakes that were symbols of the sun.

Preparation time: 15 minutes, plus chilling
Cooking time: 45 minutes–1 hour

250 g (8 oz) plain flour
125 g (4 oz) rice flour or ground rice
125 g (4 oz) caster sugar, plus extra for dusting
pinch of salt
250 g (8 oz) unsalted butter

1 Heat the oven to 150°C (300°F), Gas Mark 2.

2 Sift the two flours (or flour and rice), sugar and salt into a mixing bowl. Soften the butter slightly, cut it up, and rub it into the dry ingredients with your fingers. When the mixture starts to bind, gather it together with one hand into a ball. Knead it on a lightly floured board until it is a soft, smooth, and pliable dough.

3 Put a 20 cm (8 inch) flan ring on a greased baking sheet and put in the dough, pressing it out evenly with your knuckles to fit the ring. With the back of a knife, mark the shortbread into triangles. Prick right through to the baking sheet with a fork in a neat pattern. Cover and chill for at least 1 hour before baking, to firm it up.

4 Bake in the oven for 45 minutes–1 hour, or until the shortbread is a pale biscuit colour but still soft. Remove the shortbread from the oven and leave to cool and shrink before removing the ring, then dust lightly with caster sugar. When cold, cut into triangles and store in an airtight container.

Makes 6–8

amaretti

These macaroons are made in various sizes, and in Italy are used in many ways – small ones for petit fours and decoration, larger ones crushed and beaten into cream icing and dessert creams.

Preparation time: 30 minutes
Cooking time: 20 minutes

125 g (4 oz) ground almonds
15 g (½ oz) ground rice or rice flour
250 g (8 oz) caster sugar
¼ teaspoon ratafia or almond
  essence
2 egg whites
2 sheets of rice paper
12 blanched almonds, split
1 egg white, beaten, for glazing

1 Heat the oven to 180°C (350°F), Gas Mark 4.

2 Mix together the ground almonds, ground rice or rice flour and caster sugar. Add the almond essence to the unbeaten egg whites and mix into the dry ingredients. Cream to a smooth paste (an electric blender will save time). Put the mixture into a piping bag with a plain 1 cm (½ inch) nozzle. Rule the rice paper into 2.5–3.5 cm (1–1½ inch) squares and place on baking sheets. Pipe the mixture in the centre of each square making biscuits 2.5 cm (1 inch) in diameter and flatten slightly.

3 Press a split almond in the centre of each macaroon. Brush lightly with the beaten egg white. Bake in the oven for about 20 minutes or until golden brown. Cool on a wire rack and cut off the rice paper round each macaroon. Store in an airtight container.

Makes 40

danish cookies

Preparation time: 20 minutes, plus chilling
Cooking time: 8–10 minutes

1 Heat the oven to 200°C (400°F), Gas Mark 6.

2 Melt the butter or margarine with the sugar and syrup. Remove from the heat and stir in the almonds, chopped peel, cloves, cinnamon and ginger. Dissolve the bicarbonate of soda in a little boiling water, stir into the syrup mixture and leave to cool. Sift and knead in the flour. Form the dough into two rolls, wrap in aluminium foil or clingfilm and refrigerate for 24 hours.

3 Grease two baking sheets. Cut the rolls of dough into slices 5 mm (¼ inch) thick. Place on the baking sheets, allowing room for spreading, and bake for 8–10 minutes. Remove from the baking sheets with a palette knife and leave to cool on a wire rack.

Makes 40

250 g (8 oz) butter or margarine
200 g (7 oz) sugar
125 g (4 oz) golden syrup
75 g (3 oz) blanched almonds,
  chopped
75 g (3 oz) candied lemon peel,
  chopped
½ teaspoon ground cloves
2 teaspoons ground cinnamon
½ teaspoon ground ginger
½ teaspoon bicarbonate of soda
500 g (1 lb) plain flour

melomakarona

The intense flavour of these Greek honey biscuits actually improves with time. The biscuits are flavoured with honey, orange, brandy, cinnamon and cloves and are traditionally made for Christmas. Melomakarona are ideal served after dinner with coffee.

Preparation time: 30 minutes, plus resting and cooling
Cooking time: 30 minutes

300 ml (½ pint) light olive oil
75 g (3 oz) sugar
250 ml (8 fl oz) orange juice
375–500 g (12 oz–1 lb) plain flour
2½ teaspoons baking powder
125 ml (4 fl oz) brandy
175 g (6 oz) semolina
grated rind of 1 orange
grated rind of 1 lemon
1 teaspoon ground cloves
½ teaspoon ground cinnamon

Honey syrup:
250 g (8 oz) sugar
250 g (8 oz) honey
475 ml (16 fl oz) water
1 large piece of orange peel
1 large piece of lemon peel
125 g (4 oz) coarsely ground
  walnuts
2 teaspoons ground cloves

1   Beat the olive oil and sugar together in a large bowl, using an electric mixer. Then add the orange juice. In a separate bowl, mix 250 g (8 oz) of the flour with the baking powder. Gradually beat the flour mixture into the oil and orange juice mixture. Beat in the brandy, semolina, orange and lemon rind, cloves and cinnamon.

2   Turn the mixture out on to a floured surface and start kneading, adding more flour as necessary, until you obtain a soft and elastic dough. Cover the dough with clingfilm and let it rest for about 25 minutes.

3   Heat the oven to 180°C (350°F), Gas Mark 4.

4   Break off pieces of dough about the size of a tablespoon, roll them in your hands, then shape them into oval biscuits about 5 cm (2 inches) long. Press the tines of a fork lightly on the top of each biscuit to make a decorative pattern. Place them on a baking sheet and bake for about 20–25 minutes, until light brown. Cool on a wire rack.

5   The next day, make the honey syrup. In a saucepan, combine the sugar, honey and water and bring to a boil. Add the orange and lemon peels and simmer for 5–10 minutes to let the flavours blend. Turn the heat to low to keep the syrup liquid. Place two or three biscuits on a large slotted spoon and dip them into the syrup. Do not let them soak in it – they should absorb only a little syrup and remain crunchy.

6   Place a layer of honey-dipped biscuits on a dish. Combine the walnuts with the ground cloves, then sprinkle the mixture over the biscuits. Repeat with all of the biscuits. Let the biscuits cool completely before serving.

Makes 60–70

christmas tree cookies

These delightful biscuits originate in Scandinavia.

Preparation time: 20 minutes, plus chilling
Cooking time: about 25 minutes

75 g (3 oz) black treacle
125 g (4 oz) butter or margarine
4 cardamom pods
50 g (2 oz) caster sugar
2 tablespoons ground almonds
200 g (7 oz) plain flour
½ teaspoon bicarbonate of soda
½ teaspoon ground cinnamon
½ teaspoon ground ginger
1 egg yolk

Glacé icing:
75 g (3 oz) icing sugar, sifted
1 egg white

1 Heat the oven to 190°C (375°F), Gas Mark 5.

2 Melt the black treacle and butter or margarine in a saucepan. Split the cardamom pods open and crush the kernels finely. Add to the melted mixture with the sugar and almonds.

3 Sift the flour, bicarbonate of soda and spices into the mixture, add the egg yolk and work together to form a smooth dough. Wrap in aluminium foil and chill for 20 minutes.

4 Roll the dough out thinly on a lightly floured surface or between two sheets of clingfilm to about 5 mm (¼ inch) thick. Using biscuit cutters, cut into shapes such as stars, Christmas trees, bells and crescents about 5–6 cm (2–2½ inches) in diameter. Place on greased baking sheets and bake in the oven for about 10–12 minutes or until just firm to the touch.

5 Immediately make a hole at the top of each cookie with a skewer. When firm enough to move, transfer to a wire rack and leave until cold.

6 To make the icing, add sufficient icing sugar to the egg white to give a smooth consistency which will thinly coat the back of a metal spoon. Spread over half of the cookies making sure the holes do not become clogged with icing. Add more icing sugar to the remaining icing to thicken it slightly. Place in a piping bag fitted with a small plain nozzle and pipe a line around the remaining cookies, about 5 mm (¼ inch) from the edge. Leave to dry and store carefully in an airtight container.

7 Carefully thread a piece of ribbon or coloured string through the holes in the cookies, tie firmly and hang on the Christmas tree. If they are to be eaten they must be removed from the tree after several hours, but they may be left there indefinitely for decoration, but must be thrown away after the Christmas holidays.

Makes about 20

gingerbread family

Gingerbread people have delighted children of all ages for centuries and were originally made for fairs. This recipe is based on a traditional one as it uses honey instead of golden syrup.

Preparation time: 20 minutes, plus standing and cooling
Cooking time: 12–15 minutes

100 g (3½ oz) margarine
100 g (3½ oz) clear honey
140 g (4½ oz) caster sugar
1½ teaspoons ground ginger
½ teaspoon ground allspice
¼ teaspoon ground cinnamon
1 teaspoon cocoa powder
500 g (1½ lb) plain flour
1 teaspoon bicarbonate of soda
pinch of salt
2 eggs

Icing:
1 egg white
175–250 g (6–8 oz) icing sugar
75 g (3 oz) plain chocolate, melted

To decorate:
blanched almonds
pistachio nuts
glacé cherries
raisins

1 Stir the margarine, honey, sugar, spices and cocoa powder together and warm over a low heat until the sugar is completely dissolved. Leave to cool.

2 Sift the flour and bicarbonate of soda into a bowl and knead in the salt, eggs and honey mixture, to obtain a smooth dough. Cover and leave to stand overnight at room temperature.

3 Heat the oven to 200°C (400°F), Gas Mark 6. Grease 2 baking sheets. Roll out the dough to 5 mm (¼ inch) thick and cut out figures using a gingerbread cutter. Place on the baking sheets and bake for 12–15 minutes in the centre of the oven. Remove from the baking sheets while still warm and cool on a wire rack.

4 To make the icing, whisk the egg white stiffly with the sifted icing sugar. Decorate the figures with the piped icing, melted chocolate and the nuts and dried fruits.

Makes 12

almond sandwich cookies

Preparation time: 40 minutes, plus chilling
Cooking time: 15 minutes

4 hard-boiled egg yolks
200 g (7 oz) butter, softened
75 g (3 oz) icing sugar
few drops of vanilla essence
pinch of salt
300 g (10 oz) plain flour, sifted
125 g (4 oz) almonds
100 g (3½ oz) caster sugar
2 egg yolks
6 tablespoons redcurrant jelly or
  cherry jam
icing sugar, for sprinkling

1 Heat the oven to 200°C (400°F), Gas Mark 6.

2 Press the hard-boiled egg yolks through a sieve and beat with the butter and sifted icing sugar until well mixed. Add the vanilla essence, salt and sifted flour and mix all the ingredients to a firm dough. Wrap in aluminium foil or clingfilm, and leave for 2 hours in the refrigerator.

3 Blanch the almonds in boiling water, peel and chop coarsely, then toss in the sugar.

4 Roll out the dough to a thickness of 3 mm (⅛ inch) and, using a ring-shaped biscuit cutter, cut out circles about 5 cm (2 inches) in diameter. Beat the egg yolks, brush one side of the circles, and sprinkle the sugared almond mixture over them.

5 Place the cookies on a baking sheet with the almond mixture side uppermost and bake for 10–15 minutes.

6 Remove with a palette knife and cool on a wire rack.

7 Sandwich the circles together with redcurrant jelly or cherry jam and sprinkle with sifted icing sugar.

Makes 25

kourambiedes

These delicate morsels pierced with a clove and coated with icing sugar are sometimes known as Greek shortbreads. They are traditionally prepared at Christmas in Greece. Originally kourambiedes were made with olive oil instead of butter, but butter is more common today.

Preparation time: 40 minutes
Cooking time: 30 minutes

250 g (8 oz) butter, softened
75 g (3 oz) caster sugar
1 egg yolk
375 g (12 oz) plain flour, sifted
50 g (2 oz) finely chopped almonds
whole cloves
icing sugar, sifted

1   Heat the oven to 150°C (300°F), Gas Mark 2.

2   Cream the butter with the sugar until light and fluffy. Add the egg yolk and beat well. Stir in the flour alternately with the almonds. Knead the mixture lightly and form into a ball. Roll small pieces of dough into balls the size of hazelnuts, and press a whole clove into the centre of each one.

3   Place on a greased baking sheet and bake for 25–30 minutes.

4   While still warm, toss in icing sugar and serve.

Makes about 70

viennese crescents

To store the biscuits, place in layers between wax paper in an airtight container; this will prevent breakage.

Preparation time: 30 minutes, plus chilling
Cooking time: 10 minutes

50 g (2 oz) blanched almonds
50 g (2 oz) hazelnuts or pecans
300 g (10 oz) plain flour, sifted
75 g (3 oz) caster sugar
pinch of salt
200 g (7 oz) butter, cut into flakes
2 egg yolks
75 g (3 oz) vanilla sugar
25 g (1 oz) icing sugar, sifted

1 Heat the oven to 190°C (375°F), Gas Mark 5.

2 Finely grate the almonds and hazelnuts or pecans. Place the sifted flour in a mixing bowl with the nuts, sugar, salt, butter and egg yolks, and knead to a soft dough. Wrap in aluminium foil or clingfilm and leave for 2 hours in the refrigerator.

3 Form the dough a little at a time into cylinders the thickness of a pencil. Cut the rolls into 5 cm (2 inch) pieces and curve into crescent shapes. Bake in the centre of the oven for 10 minutes, until golden. Mix the vanilla sugar with the sifted icing sugar and toss the bicuits in this while still warm.

Makes 50

cinnamon stars

Preparation time: 50 minutes, plus cooling
Cooking time: 15–20 minutes

4 small egg whites
250 g (8 oz) icing sugar, sifted
300 g (10 oz) ground almonds
1½ tablespoons ground cinnamon
grated rind of ½ lemon
caster sugar, for sprinkling

1 Put the egg whites into a heatproof bowl. Whisk until frothy, then add the sifted icing sugar. Place over a saucepan of simmering water and continue whisking until the meringue is thick and holds its shape. Remove the bowl from the saucepan. Put 3–4 tablespoons of the meringue to one side. Fold the ground almonds, cinnamon and lemon rind into the remaining meringue mixture, and leave to cool for 1 hour.

2 Heat the oven to 160°C (325°F), Gas Mark 3. Grease and flour two baking sheets.

3 Sprinkle a work surface with caster sugar and roll out the mixture until about 5 mm (¼ inch) thick. The mixture will be soft and must be rolled out very carefully. Cut into stars with a biscuit cutter and place on the baking sheets. Spread the reserved meringue carefully over the stars and bake for 15–20 minutes, until just firm. Transfer carefully to a wire rack and leave to cool.

Makes 20

swedish yule biscuits

Some of the cinnamon and sugar mixture will fall on to the baking sheet when the biscuits are sprinkled with it. Before baking remove this with a pastry brush, so it does not burn.

Preparation time: 20 minutes, plus chilling
Cooking time: 8–10 minutes

250 g (8 oz) butter, softened
125 g (4 oz) caster sugar
1 egg
425 g (14 oz) plain flour
1 teaspoon baking powder
½ teaspoon salt
1 egg white, beaten
¼ teaspoon ground cinnamon
50 g (2 oz) sugar

1 Beat the butter with the sugar and egg until light and fluffy. Sift the flour with the baking powder and mix in the salt. Gradually add the flour to the butter mixture and knead together. Form the dough into a ball, wrap in aluminium foil or clingfilm, and leave for 3 hours in the refrigerator.

2 Heat the oven to 200°C (400°F), Gas Mark 6. Divide the dough into three portions and knead each one in turn. Take each portion of dough from the refrigerator as required and roll out to a thickness of 3 mm (⅛ inch) on a floured board. Cut out 6 cm (2½ inch) round biscuits and place on a baking sheet. Mix the cinnamon with the sugar.

3 Brush the biscuits with beaten egg white and sprinkle generously with the cinnamon and sugar mixture. Bake them for 8–10 minutes then cool the biscuits on a wire rack.

Makes 40

chocolate macaroons

Macaroons are small round cakes, crunchy on the outside and soft inside. The recipe originally came from Italy during the Renaissance: the name is derived from the Italian macherone and the Venetian macarone, meaning 'fine paste'. French macaroons are also world famous.

Preparation time: 30 minutes
Cooking time: 15–20 minutes

4 egg whites
200 g (7 oz) caster sugar
250 g (8 oz) ground almonds
125 g (4 oz) plain chocolate, grated

1 Line a baking sheet with nonstick baking paper or rice paper. Heat the oven to 180°C (350°F), Gas Mark 4.

2 Whisk the egg whites until stiff. Add the sugar gradually and continue whisking until the mixture is thick and glossy. Fold in the ground almonds and grated chocolate. Drop spoonfuls of the mixture on to the baking sheet, leaving space between each biscuit. Bake for 15–20 minutes. Do not let the macaroons become too dark or they will taste bitter.

3 Cool on the baking sheet, then carefully peel the macaroons off the nonstick baking paper or cut around each biscuit on the edible rice paper.

Makes 30

norwegian christmas rings

Preparation time: 20 minutes, plus chilling
Cooking time: 10–12 minutes

3 eggs
1 egg yolk
165 g (5½ oz) icing sugar, sifted
250 g (8 oz) butter, softened
few drops of vanilla essence
375 g (12 oz) plain flour, sifted
1 egg yolk, beaten with
  2 teaspoons water
sugar crystals, for sprinkling

1 Boil the eggs for 10–12 minutes, plunge into cold water and shell. Press the yolks through a fine sieve and stir into the egg yolk with the sifted icing sugar. Gradually work in the softened butter and the vanilla essence. Finally add the sifted flour and knead the ingredients to a soft dough. Wrap in aluminium foil or clingfilm and leave for 3 hours in the refrigerator.

2 Heat oven to 190°C (375°F), Gas Mark 5. Divide the dough into small pieces and form each into a roll about 10 cm (4 inches) in length. Brush the strips at each end with beaten egg yolk and join into rings. Generously brush the tops with egg yolk and sprinkle with sugar crystals. Place on a baking sheet and bake for 10–12 minutes.

3 Remove the rings from the baking sheet with a palette knife and leave to cool on a wire rack.

Makes 30

apricot rings

Preparation time: 30 minutes, plus chilling
Cooking time: 10–15 minutes

425 g (14 oz) plain flour
125 g (4 oz) caster sugar
pinch of salt
grated rind of 1 lemon
25 g (1 oz) vanilla sugar
1 egg
2 tablespoons rum
250 g (8 oz) butter, cut into flakes
icing sugar, for sprinkling
250 g (8 oz) apricot jam

1 Sift the flour into a mixing bowl. Make a well in the centre and add the sugar, salt, lemon rind, vanilla sugar, egg and rum. Dot the butter over the flour and knead all the ingredients to a soft dough. Wrap in aluminium foil or clingfilm and leave for 2 hours in the refrigerator.

2 Heat the oven to 180°C (350°F), Gas Mark 4. Roll out the dough, a little at a time, on a floured board, to a thickness of 3 mm (⅛ inch). Using plain and ring cutters of the same size, cut out equal quantities of rounds and rings. Place them on greased baking sheets and bake for 10–15 minutes.

3 Remove the rings and rounds from the baking sheet with a palette knife and leave to cool on a wire rack. Sift icing sugar generously on to the rings. Warm the jam over a low heat and spread smoothly on to the rounds. Place the rings on top. Add a little more jam to the centre of the rings and cool completely before storing in an airtight container.

Makes 20

crumbly almond hearts

Preparation time: 20 minutes, plus chilling
Cooking time: 10–12 minutes

1 Beat the butter with the sifted icing sugar and 1 egg yolk until pale and creamy. Add the ground almonds and sifted flour, and knead quickly to a firm dough. Form into a ball, wrap in aluminium foil or clingfilm, and leave for 2 hours in the refrigerator.

2 Heat the oven to 200°C (400°F), Gas Mark 6. Roll out the dough on a floured board to 5 mm (¼ inch) thick and cut out forty small heart shapes. Place on a large baking sheet. Beat the second egg yolk, brush the biscuits with this, and place two almond halves on each one. Bake for 10–12 minutes.

3 Allow the biscuits to cool slightly on the baking sheet, then remove to a wire rack, and leave until completely cool.

Makes 40

250 g (8 oz) butter, softened
125 g (4 oz) icing sugar, sifted
2 egg yolks
125 g (4 oz) ground almonds
375 g (12 oz) plain flour, sifted
40 blanched almonds, halved

sweet biscotti

These Italian, chocolate dipped, hard, sweet biscuits make a pretty gift at Christmas.

Preparation time: 30 minutes, plus chilling
Cooking time: 15 minutes

150 g (5 oz) butter
200 g (7 oz) caster sugar
few drops of vanilla essence
1 egg yolk
1 tablespoon milk
generous pinch each of ground
   cardamom and ground cinnamon
grated rind of ½ lemon
75 g (3 oz) ground almonds
150 g (5 oz) plain flour
125 g (4 oz) plain chocolate, broken
   into pieces

1 Beat the butter in a mixing bowl with the sugar and vanilla essence until pale and creamy. Add the egg yolk, milk, spices, lemon rind and almonds and knead the sifted flour into this mixture. Chill in the refrigerator for 1 hour.

2 Form the dough into rectangular blocks, about 8 cm (3½ inches) in diameter, wrap in aluminium foil, and leave in the refrigerator for 2 hours.

3 Heat the oven to 190°C (375°F), Gas Mark 5. Cut the blocks of dough into 5 mm (¼ inch) slices, place on a baking sheet and bake for 15 minutes.

4 Remove the biscuits with a palette knife and cool on a wire rack. Melt the pieces of chocolate in a small bowl over a saucepan of hot water. Dip the biscuits into the chocolate so that they are half coated diagonally and leave them to dry on wax paper.

Makes 15

coconut macaroons

Preparation time: 20 minutes, plus cooling
Cooking time: 20 minutes

5 egg whites
250 g (8 oz) icing sugar
250 g (8 oz) ground almonds
250 g (8 oz) desiccated coconut
grated rind of ½ lemon
1 tablespoon rum
icing sugar, for sprinkling
125 g (4 oz) plain chocolate, broken
  into pieces

1 Line a large baking sheet with rice paper. Heat the oven to 150°C (300°F), Gas Mark 2.

2 Whisk the egg whites until stiff. Fold in half the sifted icing sugar and the ground almonds. Add the coconut, remaining icing sugar, lemon rind and rum and work all together to a sticky dough. Put the mixture into a piping bag fitted with a large plain nozzle, and pipe walnut-sized drops on to the rice paper. Sprinkle the macaroons with icing sugar and bake in the centre of the oven for 20 minutes. They should have a golden crust on the outside but remain soft inside. Allow to cool on a wire rack.

3 Melt the chocolate in a bowl over hot water and dip a third of each macaroon in it. Leave the chocolate coating to set before serving.

Makes 30

iced pretzels

Preparation time: 40 minutes, plus chilling
Cooking time: 12–15 minutes

200 g (7 oz) butter
125 g (4 oz) icing sugar, sifted
1 egg yolk
pinch of salt
few drops of vanilla essence
300 g (10 oz) plain flour, sifted

Icing:
1 egg white
3 tablespoons rum
2 teaspoons lemon juice
200 g (7 oz) icing sugar, sifted

1 Cream the butter with the icing sugar to a smooth paste, then add the egg yolk, salt and vanilla essence. Knead in the sifted flour. Wrap the pastry dough in aluminium foil or clingfilm and refrigerate for 2 hours.

2 Heat the oven to 180°C (350°F), Gas Mark 4. Cut off one piece of pastry at a time and shape, leaving the rest in the refrigerator. Roll each piece in turn until pencil thin, to a length of 25 cm (10 inches) and shape into a pretzel. Place the shaped pretzels on a baking sheet and bake in the centre of the oven for 12–15 minutes.

3 To make the icing, mix the egg white with the rum, lemon juice and sifted icing sugar. Allow the pretzels to cool a little, then remove them from the baking sheet with a palette knife. Place on a wire rack and brush the tops as thickly as possible with the rum icing.

Makes 15

deep-fried pretzels

Preparation time: 30 minutes, plus standing
Cooking time: 30 minutes

1 Sift the flour into a bowl and make a well in the centre. Cream the yeast with the milk and a little sugar. Pour into the well and sprinkle over a little of the flour. Cover and leave to stand in a warm place for 15 minutes, until frothy.

2 Melt the margarine and beat with the rest of the sugar, the egg, salt, lemon rind and spices, until fluffy. Add to the yeast liquid and beat in the rest of the flour to obtain a soft light dough. Cover and leave to stand for a further 20 minutes.

3 Divide the dough into pieces the size of an egg and with floured hands form into balls. From the balls, roll 40 cm (16 inch) lengths and form these into pretzel shapes. Leave to stand for 15 minutes on a floured board.

4 Heat the oil for frying to 180°C (350°F). Place three pretzels at a time in the hot oil and fry until crisp and golden all over. Drain on kitchen paper and sprinkle with caster sugar while still hot.

Makes 20

500 g (1 lb) plain flour
25 g (1 oz) fresh yeast
250 ml (8 fl oz) lukewarm milk
50 g (2 oz) caster sugar
100 g (3½ oz) margarine
1 egg
½ teaspoon salt
grated rind of ½ lemon
generous pinch each of ground
   allspice and ground ginger
caster sugar, for sprinkling
oil, for deep-frying

american
ginger slices

Preparation time: 30 minutes, plus chilling
Cooking time: 15 minutes

6 whole pieces of preserved ginger
150 g (5 oz) butter or margarine
125 g (4 oz) caster sugar
1 egg
pinch of salt
½ teaspoon ground ginger
300 g (10 oz) plain flour
1 egg yolk, for glazing

1   Chop three of the whole ginger pieces very finely and thinly slice the remainder.

2   Cream the butter or margarine with the sugar, egg, salt, ground ginger and finely chopped ginger. Sift in the flour and work quickly together to obtain a smooth dough. Form into a ball, wrap in aluminium foil or clingfilm and leave for 2 hours in the refrigerator.

3   Heat the oven to 200°C (400°F), Gas Mark 6. Divide the dough into three and roll out one piece at a time on a floured board to about 5 mm (¼ inch) thick. Cut out strips about 6 x 3.5 cm (2½ x 1½ inches). Place on a baking sheet. Beat the egg yolk with a little water. Brush the biscuits with egg yolk, sprinkle with the sliced ginger, and bake in the centre of the oven for 15 minutes.

4   Remove the ginger slices from the baking sheet with a palette knife and leave to cool on a wire rack.

Makes 15

large cakes
& gâteaux

gâteau jalousie
with chantilly cream

The name of this gâteau has nothing to do with jealousy as might be thought. The wooden shutters you see on French houses are known as 'jalousies' and the pastry on top of this gâteau is cut across at regular intervals to resemble the slats of the wooden shutters.

Preparation time: 30–40 minutes, plus chilling and standing
Cooking time: 25 minutes

8 oz flaky or puff pastry
250 g (8 oz) apricot jam
50 g (2 oz) mixed crystallized and
    glacé fruits, chopped

Glaze:
1 egg, beaten
caster sugar

Chantilly cream:
125 ml (4 fl oz) double cream, plus
    3 tablespoons single cream, or
    175 ml (6 fl oz) whipping cream
1–2 teaspoons caster sugar
few drops of vanilla essence

1 Roll out the pastry into a large rectangle, 3 mm (⅛ inch) thick, and cut out a 30 cm (12 inch) square. Cut in half to make two strips 15 cm (6 inches) wide. Place one piece on a damp baking sheet and prick all over. Leaving a 2.5 cm (1 inch) border all round, spread the apricot jam evenly and fairly thickly over the pastry. Scatter over the chopped fruits.

2 Sprinkle the other piece of pastry lightly with flour and fold it in half lengthways. With a sharp knife, cut through the folded edge to a depth of 5 cm (2 inches) at regular 9 mm (⅜ inch) intervals, leaving a border all round of 2.5 cm (1 inch) uncut. Unfold the pastry carefully and brush off any loose flour. (If the dough has softened in the warm kitchen, it will be difficult to lift after slitting, so refrigerate it for 20 minutes, until stiffened.)

3 Brush the border of the bottom piece of pastry with water, carefully lift on the slashed top and press the borders together with your fingertips. Knock back the outside edges with the back of a knife and scallop them. Mark the top of the border with criss-cross lines. Leave the gâteau to relax for 20–30 minutes in a cool place, not the refrigerator. Meanwhile, preheat the oven to 230°C (450°F), Gas Mark 8.

4 Bake in the oven for 25 minutes. Brush the top with the beaten egg and dredge with caster sugar, then continue baking for a further 5 minutes or until the pastry has a golden glaze. Lift the gâteau carefully on to a wire rack to cool. When cold, cut across into six or eight slices.

5 To make the chantilly cream, whip the cream together until beginning to thicken, then add the sugar and vanilla essence and continue whipping until the cream just holds its shape. In hot weather, be careful not to overwhip. Serve the gâteau with the chantilly cream.

Serves 6–8

chestnut meringue gâteau

This big cake is a lovely party piece for sweet-toothed people. For very special occasions, it can be decorated with halved marrons glacés.

Preparation time: 1½ hours, plus chilling
Cooking time: 1½ hours

3 egg whites
175 g (6 oz) sugar

Chestnut meringue cream:
1 large egg white
125 g (4 oz) icing sugar
175 g (6 oz) unsalted butter
4 tablespoons sweetened
  chestnut purée
¼ teaspoon vanilla essence
approximately 2 teaspoons
  lemon juice

Praline:
75 g (3 oz) caster sugar
3 tablespoons water
6 tablespoons whole unblanched
  almonds

1 Heat the oven to 140°C (275°F), Gas Mark 1. Cover two baking sheets with greaseproof paper and draw two circles on each, 18 cm (7 inches) in diameter. Lightly oil the paper.

2 Beat the egg whites until stiff and dry, sift in 50 g (2 oz) of the sugar and whisk again until thick and glossy. Sift and fold in the remaining sugar, half at a time. Spoon the meringue into a large piping bag with a large rose nozzle. Pipe nine small rosettes on to the baking sheets outside the circles. Divide the remaining meringue equally between the four circles and spread it out evenly about 1 cm (½ inch) thick into four flat biscuits. Bake for about 1 hour or until crisp.

3 Meanwhile, make the chestnut meringue cream. Put the egg white and icing sugar in a bowl over a saucepan of simmering water and whisk until it forms soft peaks. Remove from the saucepan and continue whisking until cool. Cream the butter with the chestnut purée and gradually beat into the cooled meringue. If the meringue is hot, the butter will turn oily. Flavour with vanilla essence and lemon juice to taste.

4 Remove the meringues to a pastry board. Cut the greaseproof paper away between the circles. Turn the meringues upside down and peel off the paper. If they are a little sticky return them to the oven for a few minutes to dry out.

5 To make the praline, lightly oil a baking sheet. Put the sugar and water in a heavy-based saucepan and stir over a gentle heat until thoroughly dissolved. Tip in the almonds, stir once only. Bring to the boil and allow to bubble briskly until the syrup is caramel coloured and smells of toffee. The oil will seep out of the almond skins and may darken the syrup before it caramelizes so be careful, or it will not set properly. Pour the praline on to the baking sheet and spread with an oiled palette knife. When quite cold, chop coarsely. It can be stored in an airtight container.

6 Divide the chestnut meringue cream into four equal portions. Spread one portion over each of three meringue rounds and place them on top of each other with the plain one on top. Spread most of the remaining chestnut meringue cream round the sides. Spread the crushed praline on a sheet of greaseproof paper and, holding the gâteau sideways between two hands, roll it in the praline until the sides are evenly coated.

7 Place the gâteau on a plate and arrange the meringue rosettes on top, fixing each one with a dab of chestnut meringue cream. Refrigerate until required, preferably overnight.

Serves 8–10

bûche de noël

A log-shaped cake, traditionally prepared for the Christmas festivities, this cake dates from 1870 and was made by Parisien pastry cooks. It was inspired by the real logs which used to be burned in the hearth throughout Christmas. It is often called a 'Yule Log'.

Preparation time: 45 minutes
Cooking time: 25–30 minutes

4 eggs
125 g (4 oz) caster sugar, plus extra
 for dredging
65 g (2½ oz) plain flour
1 tablespoon cocoa powder
25 g (1 oz) butter, melted and
 cooled

Filling:
150 ml (¼ pint) double cream
1 tablespoon milk
250 g (8 oz) can sweetened
 chestnut purée

Crème au beurre au chocolat:
75 g (3 oz) caster sugar
4 tablespoons water
2 egg yolks
125–175 g (4–6 oz) unsalted butter
50 g (2 oz) plain chocolate, broken
 into pieces

To decorate:
icing sugar, sifted
cocoa powder, sifted
holly leaves

1 Heat the oven to 190°C (375°F), Gas Mark 5. Line a 30 x 25 cm (12 x 10 inch) Swiss roll tin with greased greaseproof paper.

2 Put the eggs and sugar into a bowl and whisk until the mixture is very thick and pale and the whisk leaves a heavy trail when lifted. Sift the flour and cocoa together twice and fold into the mixture, followed by the cooled runny butter. Turn into the prepared tin making sure there is plenty of mixture in the corners. Bake in the oven for 15–20 minutes, or until just firm and springy to the touch.

3 Unmould on to a sheet of greaseproof paper or nonstick baking paper dredged with caster sugar. Peel off the lining paper, trim the edges of the cake with a sharp knife, then roll up the cake with the sugared paper inside. Cool on a wire rack.

4 To make the filling, whip the cream and milk together until stiff, then fold the mixture into the chestnut purée Unroll the cake carefully, remove the paper, and spread it evenly with the chestnut mixture. Re-roll carefully.

5 To make the crème au beurre au chocolat, place the sugar in a heavy-based saucepan with the water and heat gently until dissolved. Bring to a boil and boil steadily for 3–4 minutes until it reaches 110°C (225°F) or until the syrup forms a thin thread. Pour the syrup in a thin stream on to the egg yolks, whisking all the time. Continue to whisk until the mixture is thick and cold. Beat the butter until soft and gradually beat in the egg mixture. Place the chocolate with 1 tablespoon water in a bowl over a saucepan of hot water and stir continuously until smooth and melted. Cool, then beat into the syrup mixture.

6 Coat the cake with the chocolate mixture; then mark with a palette knife to look like tree bark. Chill until set. Before serving, dredge lightly with cocoa powder and icing sugar, and decorate with holly leaves.

Serves 8

glacé fruit cake

Preparation time: 20 minutes
Cooking time: 2 hours 15 minutes

250 g (8 oz) butter, softened
250 g (8 oz) caster sugar
3 eggs
250 g (8 oz) self-raising wholemeal
  flour
2 teaspoons ground mace
150 g (5 oz) ground almonds
300 g (10 oz) mixed glacé fruits,
  chopped
Christmas ribbon, to decorate

Topping:
2 tablespoons Apricot Glaze
  (see page 11)
75 g (3 oz) mixed glacé fruits,
  sliced

1 Heat the oven to 160°C (325°F), Gas Mark 3. Prepare a 18 cm (7 inch) square cake tin.

2 Place the butter and sugar in a large mixing bowl and beat together with a wooden spoon until light and fluffy. Add the eggs, one at a time, beating well after each addition, until the mixture is thick and smooth. Fold in the flour, ground mace and ground almonds carefully, using a spatula, until thoroughly incorporated. Fold in the glacé fruits until evenly blended.

3 Spoon the mixture into the prepared tin, level the top and bake in the centre of the oven for about 2¼ hours or until the cake springs back when lightly pressed in the centre. Leave the cake to cool in the tin, then unmould it and remove the paper.

4 Brush the top of the cake with a little apricot glaze and arrange the sliced glacé fruits on top. Brush with the remaining glaze and leave to set. Measure and fit the ribbon around the cake and tie a bow.

Serves 10–12

mini christmas cakes

These little cakes – only 10 cm (4 inches) in diameter – make wonderful presents for people living alone, or to add to a Christmas hamper full of seasonal fare. At a special Christmas party, why not make a little cake for each pair of guests? Best of all, for the cake decorating enthusiast, they provide an opportunity to try out a number of designs on a single theme.

Preparation time: 1½ hours, plus drying
Cooking time: 1¾–2 hours

4 x 18 cm (7 inch) round silver
   cake boards
1 quantity Christmas cake
   mixture (see Merry Christmas
   Cake, page 74)
4 tablespoons Apricot Glaze
   (see page 11)
750 g (1½ lb) Marzipan
   (see page 10)
750 g (1½ lb) Royal Icing
   (see page 11)
½ quantity Fondant Moulding
   Paste (see page 10)

To decorate:
icing sugar and cornflour, for
   dusting
silver dragees (sugared almonds)
food colourings (red, yellow,
   and green)
Christmas ribbon

1 Heat the oven to 140°C (275°F), Gas Mark 1. To make the individual cake cases, cut out four 25 cm (10 inch) circles of double-thickness aluminium foil and mould each around the base and sides of a large tin can to make a 10 cm (4 inch) case. Remove the can carefully and place the cake cases on a baking sheet covered with a double thickness of brown paper.

2 Divide the cake mixture among the foil cases and smooth the tops. Place in the oven and bake for 1¾–2 hours. Remove and allow to cool slightly. Remove the foil and leave the cakes to cool completely. Brush the tops and sides of the cakes with apricot glaze, then cover with marzipan, reserving the trimmings. Leave to dry for a minimum of 24 hours. Make up the royal icing and attach each cake to a board with a little dab of it.

3 To decorate the first cake, flat-ice the top of the cake and leave to dry a little. Rough-ice the sides, swirling the peaks with a palette knife. Make a paper star to fit the cake and place it on top. Prick out the star design on top of the cake using a wooden skewer. Fill a piping bag, fitted with a star nozzle, with royal icing. Pipe along the outline of the star. Press a silver dragee into each point.

4 To decorate the second cake, rough-ice all over the cake with royal icing. Use marzipan trimmings to make holly leaves and berries and place the clusters on top of the cake.

5 To decorate the third cake, roll out half the moulding paste on a surface dusted with icing sugar and cornflour to a circle large enough to cover the top and sides of the cake with a 2.5 cm (1 inch) border. Place it centrally on the cake and smooth into place with fingers dipped in icing sugar. Trim the edges. Using a piping bag fitted with a plain nozzle, pipe 'Merry Christmas' on top of the cake in royal icing. Colour a little royal icing red and overpipe the letters. Use the moulding paste trimmings to make holly leaves and berries. Tie Christmas ribbon around the cake.

6 To decorate the final cake, roll out the remaining moulding paste and cover the cake as described for the third cake. Use the trimmings to make a red candle shape with yellow flame, green holly leaves and red berries. Finish by tying ribbon around the cake.

Serves 8

merry christmas cake

This enriched fruit cake mixture, with extra spices and brandy, makes a Christmas cake to remember.

375 g (12 oz) seedless raisins

375 g (12 oz) currants

375 g (12 oz) sultanas

175 g (6 oz) chopped mixed peel

75 g (3 oz) glacé cherries,
   quartered, washed and dried

grated rind of 1 lemon

375 g (12 oz) butter, softened

300 g (10 oz) light or dark soft
   brown sugar

4 medium or large eggs

300 g (10 oz) plain flour, sifted

pinch of salt

2 teaspoons mixed spice

½ teaspoon ground cinnamon

⅛ teaspoon grated nutmeg

3 tablespoons brandy or sherry

3–4 tablespoons brandy for
   soaking, optional

1 quantity Apricot Glaze (see
   page 11)

875 g (1¾ lb) Marzipan (see
   page 10)

1 kg (2 lb) Royal Icing (see page 11)

23 cm (9 inch) square silver cake
   board

To decorate:

4 oz white fondant moulding paste
   (optional) (see page 10)

silver ribbon

holly sprig

icing sugar, for dusting

Preparation time: about 20 minutes, plus icing and decorating
Cooking time: 3½–3¾ hours

1 Heat the oven to 150°C (300°F), Gas Mark 2. Grease and double-line a 20 cm (8 inch) square cake tin with greased greaseproof paper or nonstick baking paper.

2 Mix together the dried fruits, peel, glacé cherries and lemon rind. Cream the butter and sugar together until pale coloured. Beat in the eggs one at a time, following each with a tablespoon of flour. Sift the remaining flour with the salt and spices, and fold into the creamed mixture, followed by the brandy or sherry. Add the fruit mixture and combine the ingredients well.

3 Turn the mixture into the prepared tin, level the top, and make a slight hollow in the centre. Wrap several thicknesses of brown paper or newspaper round the outside of the tin and bake for 3½–3¾ hours or until a skewer inserted into the centre of the cake comes out clean.

4 Cool in the tin, then unmould on to a wire rack. Store in an airtight container or wrapped in aluminium foil until required. If using extra brandy, pierce the cake all over with a fine skewer and drizzle 3–4 tablespoons of brandy over it before storing.

5 To prepare the cake for decoration, brush the top and sides with apricot glaze, then cover with marzipan. Leave the marzipan to dry for a minimum of 24 hours.

6 Make the royal icing and attach the cake to the board with a dab of it. Flat-ice the sides of the cake, then spread the remainder over the top, peaking it with a palette knife. Leave to set.

7 If liked, cover the top of the cake board with moulding paste. Tie the silver ribbon around the cake and top with the holly sprig, dusted with icing sugar.

Serves 8

panforte di siena

This is the Christmas cake of Siena, Italy. At Christmas the familiar octagonal boxes of panforte can be seen in pasticcerie all over Italy, but especially in Siena where this unusual delicacy is made. Legend has it that Panforte was created as a gift for the Christ child by a young Tuscan boy who had nothing to give other than what was in his pocket – a stale piece of bread and some nuts, which he encrusted into the bread with some honey. It is the custom to eat it with an espresso coffee or a glass of sweet vin santo, at teatime.

Preparation time: 20 minutes, plus cooling
Cooking time: 50 minutes

rice paper, for lining

75 g (3 oz) hazelnuts, toasted,
  skinned and chopped

75 g (3 oz) blanched almonds,
  toasted and chopped

75 g (3 oz) candied orange peel,
  chopped

75 g (3 oz) candied lemon peel,
  chopped

75 g (3 oz) candied fruit, chopped

2 teaspoons ground cinnamon

large pinch of mixed spice

75 g (3 oz) plain flour, sifted

125 g (4 oz) thick honey

100 g (3½ oz) caster sugar

icing sugar, for dredging

1   Heat the oven to 150°C (300°F), Gas Mark 2. Line a deep sponge cake tin or a loose-bottomed 18–20 cm (7–8 inch) round cake tin with rice paper.

2   Combine the nuts, peel and fruit. Sift the spices and flour into the fruit mixture and stir until evenly mixed. Put the honey and sugar into a saucepan and bring slowly to the boil. Pour over the nut mixture and stir well until blended and forming a sticky mass.

3   Place the mixture in the tin, but don't press it down too firmly. Bake for about 50 minutes or until almost firm to the touch. Cool in the tin and then remove carefully. If the rice paper is torn or pulled away from the cake, add a new layer, attaching it with a dab of lightly beaten egg white. Dredge the top heavily with sifted icing sugar and store wrapped in aluminium foil.

4   Serve cut into thin wedges.

Serves 15

sachertorte

This is one of Vienna's most famous cakes, renowned for its lightness, which is achieved by the high proportion of egg whites. When the cake is cool, split it in half crossways and sandwich the two layers together with apricot jam. In Vienna, Sachertorte is served with whipped cream.

Preparation time: 40 minutes
Cooking time: 45–55, plus cooling and setting

165 g (5½ oz) unsalted butter,
  softened
165 g (5½ oz) sugar
7 eggs, separated, whites stiffly
  beaten
165 g (5½ oz) plain chocolate,
  broken into pieces
125 g (4 oz) plain flour, sifted
40 g (1½ oz) ground almonds
125 g (4 oz) apricot jam
icing sugar, for dusting

Chocolate icing:
100 ml (3½ fl oz) double cream
2 teaspoons brandy
125 g (4 oz) plain chocolate, broken
  into pieces

1 Heat the oven to 180°C (350°F), Gas Mark 4. Butter and line an 18 cm (7 inch) round cake tin with greaseproof paper. Brush the paper with melted butter and dust with flour.

2 Beat the butter in a mixing bowl, until it is pale and soft. Add the sugar and beat until light and fluffy. Add the egg yolks, one at a time, beating well after each addition.

3 Place the chocolate in a bowl set over hot water. When it has melted, pour it into the cake mixture and blend it in. Sift the flour and almonds into the bowl and fold into the butter mixture. Gently fold in one-third of the beaten egg whites, then fold in the rest.

4 Pour the mixture into the tin and bake for 45–55 minutes or until a skewer inserted into the centre comes out clean. Remove from the oven and leave the cake in the tin for 10 minutes before turning it out to cool completely.

5 Warm the apricot jam and spread it over the top and sides of the cake. Leave it to set. To make the icing, place the cream in a saucepan with the brandy and bring just to the boil. Add the chocolate pieces, and stir until the chocolate melts and is thick and smooth. Pour the chocolate mixture evenly over the cake and leave to set, about 15 minutes, then dust with icing sugar.

Serves 8

bishop's cake

An old English fruit cake that got its name from the stained glass window because of the appearance of each slice. It is sometimes known as American Christmas cake and it is more of a fruit and nut slab than a cake. This cake should be stored in the refrigerator, and wrapped in aluminium foil. As it is so sweet serve only thin slices; it can be served with sherry.

Preparation time: 20 minutes
Cooking time: 1¾ hours

500 g (1 lb) whole shelled Brazil
nuts
12 dates, pitted
250 g (8 oz) glacé cherries, red and
green mixed
100 g (3½ oz) plain flour
½ teaspoon baking powder
½ teaspoon salt
175 g (6 oz) caster sugar
3 eggs, beaten
1 teaspoon vanilla essence
icing sugar, for dredging

1 Heat the oven to 150°C (300°F), Gas Mark 2. Grease a 21 x 11 cm (8½ x 4¼ inch) loaf tin. Line the base and sides with greased greaseproof paper.

2 Put the nuts, whole dates and whole glacé cherries into a large mixing bowl. Sift the dry ingredients over them and mix thoroughly. Pour in the eggs and vanilla. Stir well and spoon into the prepared tin. Bake for about 1¾ hours or until a skewer inserted in the centre comes out clean.

3 Remove from the tin, peel away the paper, and cool completely on a wire rack. Wrap in aluminium foil and store in the refrigerator. It will keep for up to 3 weeks. Serve dredged with icing sugar.

Serves 10–12

festive light christmas cake

If you place brown paper around the outside of the cake tin before baking, it will prevent the edges of the cake becoming brown and overcooked before the inside is cooked through. The undecorated cake will keep well if wrapped in wax paper and stored in an airtight container.

Preparation time: 1 hour
Cooking time: 3–3½ hours

250 g (8 oz) butter

250 g (8 oz) caster sugar

¼ teaspoon vanilla essence

generous pinch of salt

1 tablespoon rum

6 eggs

375 g (12 oz) plain flour

1 teaspoon baking powder

425 g (14 oz) sultanas

50 g (2 oz) ground almonds

125 g (4 oz) candied lemon peel,
   chopped

125 g (4 oz) blanched almonds,
   halved

Glaze and decoration:

2 tablespoons sugar

4 tablespoons water

2 tablespoons apricot jam

250 g (8 oz) almond paste

food colourings

egg white, for sticking

1　Heat the oven to 150°C (300°F), Gas Mark 2. Line a 23 cm (9 inch) round cake tin with greased greaseproof paper.

2　Beat the butter with the caster sugar, vanilla essence, salt and rum until pale and creamy. Stir in the eggs one at a time. If the eggs should curdle the mixture slightly, add a tablespoon of the flour. Sift the remaining flour with the baking powder and mix with the sultanas, ground almonds and chopped peel. Fold this flour mixture gradually into the creamed mixture. Turn into the prepared tin, smooth the surface with the back of a wet spoon and arrange the almond halves in a circular pattern on top.

3　Bake the cake for 3–3½ hours. Before removing from the oven test with a skewer; if the skewer comes out clean from the centre, then the cake is cooked through. Allow to stand in the tin for about 15 minutes then place on a wire cooling rack, leaving the greaseproof paper on the cake.

4　Heat the sugar and water, stirring continuously until the sugar is completely dissolved. Boil for 2–3 minutes. Cover the top of the cake with this glaze and leave to cool.

5　Spread the sides of the cake with the warmed jam. Roll out the almond paste thinly and cut pieces to cover the sides of the cake, cutting into strips at the top. Colour the rest of the marzipan with the food colouring of your choice, cut out Christmas tree shapes and attach to the cake with unbeaten egg white.

Serves 16–18

vasilopitta

This is the New Year's cake served at the stroke of midnight on New Year's Eve in Greece. St. Basil is the patron saint of Greece so the cake is also named for him. It is usually much larger than this version and always has a lucky coin baked into it, although the ingredients do vary from family to family. When it is cut, a piece is offered to the Holy Mother and St. Basil, and the rest cut up for the assembled gathering. Any left over is supposed to be given to the poor on the following day. If the lucky coin is in the piece left for St. Basil, then everyone should have a happy year, and if in the leftovers, then the poor will benefit. Wrap the coin in aluminium foil before placing it in the mixture.

Preparation time: 30 minutes
Cooking time: 50 minutes–1 hour

375 g (12 oz) plain flour
1 tablespoon baking powder
1 teaspoon ground nutmeg
250 g (8 oz) unsalted butter
500 g (1 lb) caster sugar
4 large eggs
250 ml (8 fl oz) orange juice
grated rind of 1 large orange
flaked or blanched almonds, to
  decorate

1 Heat the oven to 180°C (350°F), Gas Mark 4. Line a roasting tin, approximately 30 x 25 x 5 cm (12 x 10 x 2 inches), with greased greaseproof paper.

2 Sift the flour, baking powder and nutmeg together. Cream the butter and sugar until very light and fluffy; beat in the eggs, one at a time, following each with a spoonful of flour; then beat in about one-third of the flour. Gradually beat in the orange juice, alternating with the remaining flour and the orange rind, until smooth and evenly blended. Drop in the coin if using.

3 Turn into the prepared tin and either sprinkle with flaked almonds or write the New Year's date on top of the cake with blanched almonds. Bake for 50 minutes–1 hour until the cake is golden brown and just firm to the touch. Unmould carefully on to a wire rack and leave to cool. Serve cut into squares or diamonds.

Serves 10–12

gingerbread cottage

Preparation time: 1 hour
Cooking time: 15–20 minutes

175 g (6 oz) clear honey
65 g (2½ oz) black treacle
65 g (2½ oz) unsalted butter
625 g (1¼ lb) plain flour
1½ teaspoons bicarbonate of soda
1 tablespoon ground ginger
1 egg
2 egg yolks

To decorate:
500 g (1 lb) Royal Icing (see
    page 11)
28–30 cm (11–12 inch) square silver
    cake board
250 g (8 oz) fondant moulding
    paste (see page 10)
white and pink marshmallows
selection of small sweets (such as
    dolly mixtures, jellies)
icing sugar, for dusting

1   Heat the honey, black treacle and butter in a small saucepan until the butter
    has melted. Sift the flour, bicarbonate of soda and ginger into a bowl. Add
    the egg and the yolks to the melted mixture and mix to a dough. Wrap and
    chill for 30 minutes.

2   Grease two large baking sheets. Heat the oven to 180°C (350°F), Gas Mark 4.
    Roll out the dough on a floured surface and cut out two 15.5 x 10.5 cm
    (6¼ x 4¼ inch) rectangles to make the roof. Cut out two 14 x 8 cm (5½ x 3¼
    inch) rectangles for the sides. Cut out two 14 cm (5½ inch) squares for the
    cottage ends. From each end piece cut a sloping roof from the centre of one
    side to half way down two opposite sides. Transfer the sections to the baking
    sheets. Cut out windows and a door, then transfer them to a baking sheet to
    bake. Cut out small shutters from the trimmings, two for each window. Bake
    all the sections for 10–15 minutes until beginning to colour around the
    edges. Transfer to a wire rack to cool.

3   Spoon some royal icing into a piping bag fitted with a writing nozzle. Spread
    more icing over the cake board. Secure the sides and ends of the cottage to
    the board using more icing to glue the sections together at the corners.
    Spread the top edges with more icing and secure the roof sections. Leave
    for about 2 hours to set.

4   Spread a little more icing over the roof sections. Roll out the fondant
    moulding paste to a rectangle and use to cover the roof. Use the trimmings
    to shape a chimney and little snow drifts around the cottage. Pipe little
    icicles around the edges of the roof with icing in the piping bag.

5   Secure the shutters and door using icing in the bag. Use the marshmallows
    and candies to decorate the cottage, cutting if necessary into small pieces.
    Lightly dust the cottage and board with icing sugar.

Serves 10

epiphany cake

The baking of special cakes to celebrate Epiphany or Twelfth Night on 6 January is an old custom which has its origins in the Roman Saturnalia (the feast in honour of the god Saturn). This festival of gluttony, in which everyone could take part, was carried over into early Christian Europe. One ingredient of the feast was the choosing of a king. A bean was hidden in a cake and whoever found it became king for a day. The custom of including a bean in a cake – or a coin – still survives today. In Switzerland the custom of Epiphany cake was revived after the Second World War and has remained popular.

Preparation time: 40 minutes, plus proving
Cooking time: 35–40 minutes

500 g (1 lb) strong plain flour
25 g (1 oz) fresh yeast or 15 g (½ oz) dried yeast
300 ml (½ pint) lukewarm milk
125 g (4 oz) butter
75 g (3 oz) caster sugar
1 teaspoon salt
grated rind of 1 lemon
pinch of grated nutmeg
2 eggs
125 g (4 oz) raisins
50 g (2 oz) blanched almonds, chopped
1 tablespoon rum
1 egg yolk, to glaze

1 Sift the flour into a bowl and make a well in the centre. Combine the yeast and milk, leave for 10 minutes or until frothy, then pour into the well. Sprinkle the mixture with flour, cover the bowl with a damp cloth, and leave for 15 minutes.

2 Melt the butter and beat with the sugar, salt, lemon rind, nutmeg and eggs. Add to the bowl while still warm and work all the ingredients together to make smooth dough. Knead for 10 minutes or until the dough is smooth and elastic. Cover the bowl and leave to rise for 1–1½ hours.

3 Meanwhile, sprinkle the raisins and almonds with the rum and leave to soak. Knead quickly into the risen dough. Divide the dough into two and shape one half into a flattened ball. Place the dough on a lightly greased baking sheet. Divide the remaining dough into seven pieces and shape these into balls.

4 Dilute the egg yolk with a little water. Brush the mixture over the large piece of dough, place the smaller ones around it and then glaze them too. Cover with oiled clingfilm and leave to rise for 45 minutes, or until doubled in size, then brush once more with egg yolk. Meanwhile heat the oven to 200°C (400°F), Gas Mark 6. Bake in the oven for 35 minutes or until done.

Serves 15

bienenstich

Preparation time: 40 minutes
Cooking time: 40 minutes

1 Heat oven to 190°C (375°F), Gas Mark 5. Grease a 20 cm (8 inch) loose-bottomed cake tin.

2 Sift together the flour, baking powder and salt. Cream the butter and sugar until light and fluffy. Combine the milk and egg and gradually add to the creamed mixture. Work in the dry ingredients to make a soft dough. Press the dough evenly over the bottom of the cake tin.

3 To make the topping, melt the butter in a saucepan over low heat, add the sugar, and stir until combined. Remove from the heat, stir in the almonds and vanilla, and allow to cool. Spread over the dough. Bake for 40 minutes. Cool on a wire rack.

4 To make the filling, cream the butter and sugar together until light and fluffy, then gradually beat in the cold custard or vanilla dessert and the vanilla essence. When cold, split the cake into two layers horizontally and sandwich together with the filling.

Serves 8–10

200 g (7 oz) plain flour
2 teaspoons baking powder
pinch of salt
75 g (3 oz) butter
75 g (3 oz) caster sugar
2 tablespoons milk
1 egg

Topping:
75 g (3 oz) butter
125 g (4 oz) sugar
125 g (4 oz) blanched slivered
  almonds
1 teaspoon vanilla essence

Filling:
250 g (8 oz) butter
4 tablespoons caster sugar
250 g (8 oz) thick cold egg custard
2 teaspoons vanilla essence

finnish sour cream cake

Preparation time: 20 minutes
Cooking time: 1¼ hours

1 Heat the oven to 180°C (350°F), Gas Mark 4. Grease a 23 cm (9 inch) ring mould and dust with sugar.

2 Place the eggs, soured cream, sugar and almond essence in a bowl and mix until combined. Sift the flour with the bicarbonate of soda, salt and spices and add gradually to the egg mixture, beating until the mixture is smooth. Pour into the ring mould. Bake in the oven for 1¼ hours or until a skewer inserted in the centre comes out clean. Leave in the mould for 10 minutes before unmoulding to cool on a wire rack.

Serves 8–10

2 eggs, beaten
450 ml (¾ pint) soured cream
500 g (1 lb) caster sugar
3 drops of almond essence
375 g (12 oz) plain flour
1 teaspoon bicarbonate of soda
½ teaspoon salt
1 teaspoon cinnamon
1 teaspoon ground cardamom

tropical christmas cake

Preparation time: 30 minutes
Cooking time: 1½ hours

300 g (10 oz) unsalted butter
250 g (8 oz) caster sugar
3 large eggs, beaten
375 g (12 oz) self-raising flour or
    plain flour with 2 teaspoons
    baking powder added
75 g (3 oz) glacé cherries
75 g (3 oz) mixed peel
40 g (1½ oz) angelica
50 g (2 oz) walnuts
425 g (14 oz) can pineapple rings,
    in syrup
40 g (1½ oz) desiccated coconut
125 g (4 oz) sultanas

Icing:
40 g (1½ oz) unsalted butter
175 g (6 oz) icing sugar
25 g (1 oz) desiccated coconut
toasted coconut shavings, to
    decorate

1 Heat the oven to 160°C (325°F), Gas Mark 3. Grease and flour a 1.5 litre
   (2½ pint) ring mould or a 20 cm (8 inch) cake tin.

2 Cream the butter and sugar until soft and light. Gradually beat in the eggs.
   Sift the flour and fold into the creamed mixture.

3 Chop the glacé cherries, mixed peel, angelica and walnuts. Drain the
   canned pineapple, setting aside 3 tablespoons of syrup for the icing and
   7 tablespoons of syrup for the cake. Chop the pineapple rings finely. Fold all
   the chopped ingredients, including the pineapple, into the cake mixture with
   the coconut, sultanas and the reserved 7 tablespoons of pineapple syrup.

4 Put the mixture into the ring mould or cake tin. Bake in the oven for
   1¼ hours if using a ring mould and 1½ hours if using a 20 cm (8 inch) tin.
   Cool for at least 10 minutes in the tin, then unmould carefully, and allow
   to cool completely.

5 To make the icing, melt the butter in a saucepan and remove from the heat.
   Sift the icing sugar into the butter, then add the reserved pineapple syrup
   and the desiccated coconut. Stir to combine, spread over the top of the
   cake and a little down the sides. Scatter with toasted coconut shavings.

Serves 10

variation: rich fruit cake

1 Omit the canned pineapple rings, desiccated coconut and pineapple syrup.
   Use moist brown sugar instead of the caster sugar, and use plain flour,
   omitting the baking powder. Add 2 more eggs (5 in total), 875 g (1¾ lb)
   mixed dried fruit and 2 tablespoons of sherry.

2 Bake in a slightly cooler oven at 150°C (300°F), Gas Mark 2 for 1¾ hours.
   Reduce the heat to 140°C (275°F), Gas Mark 1 and bake for a further
   1 hour. Cool for at least 10 minutes in the tin, then unmould very carefully
   and cool further on a wire rack.

brussels fruit cake

Preparation time: 40 minutes, plus standing and cooling
Cooking time: 2–2¼ hours

200 g (7 oz) crystallised pineapple
200 g (7 oz) crystallised pears
75 g (3 oz) candied lemon peel
275 g (9 oz) red and green glacé
  cherries, halved
250 g (8 oz) walnuts, finely
  chopped
125 g (4 oz) pecans, finely chopped
125 g (4 oz) almonds, finely
  chopped
125 g (4 oz) hazelnuts or
  macadamias, finely chopped
425 g (14 oz) raisins
5 tablespoons sherry, plus extra
  for moistening
250 g (8 oz) butter
500 g (1 lb) caster sugar
pinch each of salt and grated
  nutmeg
6 eggs
500 g (1 lb) self-raising flour
crystallised and glacé fruit, to
  decorate

1 Finely dice the pineapple, pears and candied peel, and mix with the cherries, nuts, raisins and sherry. Leave to stand overnight.

2 Heat the oven to 160°C (325°F), Gas Mark 3. Line two 1 kg (2 lb) loaf tins with buttered greaseproof paper.

3 Beat the butter with the sugar, salt and nutmeg until pale and creamy, then beat in the eggs one at a time. Fold in the sifted flour and finally stir in the fruit-and-nut mixture. Turn into the prepared tins and bake for 2–2¼ hours.

4 Remove the cakes from the loaf tins when cool and strip off the greaseproof paper. Wrap each cake in cheesecloth moistened in sherry, then wrap in aluminium foil, and leave in the refrigerator for 4 weeks. Every week, moisten the cheesecloth with sherry again. Finally, decorate the cakes with candied fruits.

Serves 12–15

christmas night gâteau

Preparation time: 40 minutes
Cooking time: 50 minutes

Sponge:

4 eggs, separated
3 tablespoons water
175 g (6 oz) caster sugar
1 tablespoon vanilla sugar
150 g (5 oz) plain flour
100 g (3½ oz) cornflour
2 teaspoons baking powder

Filling and topping:

600 ml (1 pint) double cream
150 g (5 oz) caster sugar
40 g (1½ oz) cocoa powder
1 tablespoon boiling water
1 tablespoon rum
5 g (¼ oz) powdered gelatine
2 tablespoons water
3 tablespoons cranberry jelly

Decoration:

125 g (4 oz) plain chocolate
8 glacé cherries, halved
1 teaspoon icing sugar
25 g (1 oz) toasted flaked almonds

1 Heat the oven to 190°C (375°F), Gas Mark 5. Grease the base of a 23 cm (9 inch) cake tin with butter or margarine.

2 Beat the egg yolks with the water, half the sugar and the vanilla sugar until pale and creamy. Whisk the egg whites in a separate bowl until stiff and fold in the remaining sugar, then carefully fold into the egg yolk mixture. Sift the flour with the cornflour and baking powder, and carefully fold into the mixture. Turn into the prepared tin, smooth the surface, and bake for 30–40 minutes. Cool on a wire rack. Leave the cake to stand overnight, if possible, then cut through twice to make three layers.

3 To make the filling, whip the cream with the sugar until stiff. Cream the cocoa powder with the boiling water and rum, cool, and mix one-quarter of the cream with it. Spread this chocolate cream thickly on the first layer of cake and place the second layer on top.

4 Dissolve the gelatine in the 2 tablespoons of water over a gentle heat. Warm the cranberry jelly, cool slightly, and mix with the dissolved gelatine, into a second quarter of the cream. Cover the second cake layer with this mixture and top with the last cake layer. Cover the cake all over with some of the remaining cream, place the rest in a piping bag fitted with a star nozzle, and sixteen rosettes around the top of the cake.

5 To decorate, melt half the chocolate by standing it in a bowl over a saucepan of hot water and spread thinly on to greaseproof paper or aluminium foil. When the chocolate has set, dip a small star-shaped cutter into hot water, and cut out sixteen star-shapes. Place a chocolate star and halved glacé cherry on each rosette. Coarsely grate the remaining chocolate. Sprinkle this over the centre of the cake, sift lightly with icing sugar, and decorate the sides of the cake with flaked almonds.

Serves 10

american fruit and nut cake

Preparation time: 30 minutes
Cooking time: about 1¾ hours

175 g (6 oz) pitted, no-need-to-
soak prunes, finely chopped
125 g (4 oz) dried apricot halves,
finely chopped
6 tablespoons dark rum
175 g (6 oz) butter or hard
margarine
175 g (6 oz) dark soft brown sugar
3 eggs
125 g (4 oz) wholemeal flour
125 g (4 oz) plain flour
¾ teaspoon baking powder
¾ teaspoon ground allspice
¼ teaspoon ground ginger
125 g (4 oz) chopped mixed nuts
(such as almonds, macadamias,
hazelnuts, walnuts, pecans)
175 g (6 oz) raisins
grated rind of 1 lemon
grated rind of 1 orange
1 tablespoon black treacle

Topping:
about 4 tablespoons redcurrant
jelly, melted
selection of shelled mixed nuts
(such as Brazils, pecans,
almonds, walnuts)
a few no-need-to-soak prunes
glacé cherries

1 Heat the oven to 150°C (300°F), Gas Mark 2. Line the sides of a 25 cm
(10 inch) springform fitted around a ring mould with two strips of nonstick
baking paper or greased greaseproof paper.

2 Put the prunes and apricots into a bowl with the rum. Leave to soak for
about 15 minutes while preparing the rest of the ingredients.

3 Cream the butter or margarine and sugar together until very light and fluffy
and pale in colour. Beat in the eggs, one at a time, following each with
1 tablespoon of wholemeal flour. Sift the plain flour with the baking powder
and spices and fold into the mixture with the remaining wholemeal flour.
Add all the other ingredients including the soaked prunes and apricots
(plus any excess liquid in the bowl) and mix well.

4 Turn into the tin and level the top. Tie a piece of newspaper, folded into
a treble thickness, around the outside of the tin. Place in the oven and
bake for about 1¾ hours or until a skewer inserted in the cake comes out
clean. Leave in the tin until cold, then remove carefully and peel off the
lining paper.

5 To make the topping, brush the cake with the redcurrant jelly then arrange
an attractive decoration of nuts, prunes and cherries on the top. Brush
again with more jelly and leave to set. This cake can be stored in an airtight
container for up to 2 weeks before use.

Serves 12

sweet breads

date and almond stollen

Stollen is a fruited yeast bread made in many parts of Germany.

Preparation time: 40 minutes, plus rising
Cooking time: 1 hour

Stollen dough:

500 g (1 lb) plain flour
25 g (1 oz) fresh yeast
250 ml (8 fl oz) lukewarm milk
50 g (2 oz) caster sugar
2 eggs
150 g (5 oz) butter, cut into flakes
50 g (2 oz) blanched almonds, chopped
grated rind of 1 lemon
pinch of salt

Filling:

25 g (1 oz) cornflour
450 ml (¾ pint) milk
1 egg yolk
100 g (3½ oz) caster sugar
250 g (8 oz) dates, finely chopped
15 g (½ oz) butter

Icing:

200 g (7 oz) icing sugar
1 egg white
4 tablespoons lemon juice
2 tablespoons toasted flaked almonds

1 Grease a baking sheet with butter or margarine. Sift the flour into a bowl and form a well in the centre. Cream the yeast with a little of the milk and 1 tablespoon of the sugar. Add the remaining milk and pour into the well in the flour. Sprinkle a little flour over it, cover, and leave to stand for 15 minutes in a warm place, until frothy.

2 Beat the eggs and mix with the remaining sugar, the butter, almonds, lemon rind and salt. Add to the flour-and-yeast mixture and knead all the ingredients well for 5–10 minutes, to form a smooth elastic dough. Cover and leave to rise for 30 minutes.

3 To make the filling, blend the cornflour with a little of the milk, the egg yolk and sugar. Bring the dates to the boil in the remaining milk. Stir the milk and dates into the cornflour mixture and then add the butter. Return to the heat and bring to the boil, stirring continuously, until thickened. Leave the mixture to cool, stirring occasionally to prevent a skin forming.

4 Lightly knead the dough and roll out to 1 cm (½ inch) thick on a floured board. Spread the date mixture evenly over it. Turn both side edges over twice toward the centre and press together. Place on the baking sheet and leave to stand for a further 20 minutes. Meanwhile, heat the oven to 200°C (400°F), Gas Mark 6.

5 Bake the stollen for 1 hour. Sift the icing sugar and beat into the egg white with the lemon juice. Ice the stollen while still warm and sprinkle flaked almonds over the icing before it sets.

Serves 8

norwegian sweet bread

In many parts of the world, beer is added to bread to give extra flavour and richness. This delicious Norwegian bread has a full flavour and a delightfully chewy texture.

Preparation time: 30 minutes, plus standing and rising
Cooking time: 40 minutes

2 tablespoons fresh yeast
300 ml (½ pint) lukewarm milk
750 g (1½ lb) plain flour
125 g (4 oz) sugar
3 teaspoons salt
½ teaspoon ground cloves
½ teaspoon black pepper
350 ml (12 fl oz) light beer
175 g (6 oz) golden syrup
250 g (8 oz) rye flour
175 g (6 oz) raisins

1   Soften the yeast in the warm milk in a large bowl and let it stand for 5 minutes. Beat in 125 g (4 oz) of the plain flour, the sugar, salt, cloves and pepper. Cover the bowl with a kitchen towel and stand in a warm place for 40 minutes or until the dough is light and bubbly.

2   Add the beer and syrup. Beat in the rye flour and raisins and enough of the remaining plain flour to make a moderately stiff dough. Turn the dough out on to a lightly floured work surface and knead until smooth and elastic, about 8–10 minutes. Place in a greased bowl, turning the dough to grease the surface. Cover and allow to rise in a warm place until doubled in size, about 1 hour. Meanwhile, grease a baking sheet.

3   Knock the dough down and rest for a further 10 minutes. Divide the dough into thirds and shape into three round loaves. Place on the baking sheet, cover, and let rise until doubled in size, for about 35–40 minutes. Meanwhile, heat the oven to 190°C (375°F), Gas Mark 5. Bake for about 40 minutes, then cool on a wire rack.

Makes 3

dresden christmas stollen

At Christmas, most families prefer the Dresden stollen which is rich and is decorated with colourful candied fruits for the occasion. This stollen tastes best when eaten fresh. However, if well wrapped in aluminium foil, it will keep for 3–4 days and when dry can be sliced and toasted.

Preparation time: 45 minutes, plus rising
Cooking time: 1 hour

75 g (3 oz) sultanas

75 g (3 oz) raisins

25 g (1 oz) flaked almonds, toasted

25 g (1 oz) glacé cherries, halved

50 g (2 oz) candied lemon peel, chopped

grated rind of 1 lemon

25 ml (1 fl oz) rum or brandy

500 g (1 lb) plain flour

pinch of salt

¼ teaspoon ground mace or grated nutmeg

25 g (1 oz) dried yeast

50 ml (2 fl oz) lukewarm milk

125 ml (4 fl oz) lukewarm water

25 g (1 oz) sugar

125 g (4 oz) butter, softened

about 40 g (1½ oz) butter, melted

To glaze:

4 tablespoons sugar

4 tablespoons boiling water

To decorate:

mixed candied fruits

citrus peel

glacé cherries

1   Put the fruit, nuts, peel and grated lemon rind in a bowl and pour the rum or brandy over them. Leave to soak, preferably overnight, until the liquor is absorbed.

2   Sift the flour, salt and spice into a warmed mixing bowl. Mix the yeast with the warm milk and water and a teaspoon of the sugar, sprinkle with flour, and leave in a warm place until the crust cracks. Stir the yeast mixture into the flour with the remaining sugar and mix into a dough. Beat in the softened butter. Turn the dough on to a floured board and knead for 10 minutes until smooth and no longer sticky.

3   Cover the dough and leave in a warm place for 30 minutes or until doubled in size. Punch it down, and work in the fruit, one-third at a time. Do this quickly or the dough will discolour. Shape into an oval. Roll out to about 2.5 cm (1 inch) thick. Make a dent lengthways with the rolling pin, slightly off-centre. Fold the narrower side over on to the wide side and press down. Place the stollen on a greased baking sheet, cover, and leave in a warm place to prove for about 20 minutes or until puffy. Meanwhile, heat the oven to 230°C (450°F), Gas Mark 8.

4   Brush the stollen with melted butter and bake in the preheated hot oven for 30 minutes. Reduce the heat to 200°C (400°F), Gas Mark 6 and continue baking for a further 20–30 minutes. A skewer inserted should come out clean when the stollen is cooked.

5   Dissolve the sugar in the water for the glaze. While the stollen is still hot, brush with sugar glaze. When decorating for Christmas, arrange mixed candied fruit on top of the stollen and brush again with the sugar glaze.

Serves 8–10

swedish coffee breads

Preparation time: 40 minutes, plus standing and rising
Cooking time: 15–20 minutes

50 g (2 oz) butter
500 g (1 lb) plain flour
75 g (3 oz) caster sugar
pinch of salt
25 g (1 oz) fresh yeast
250 ml (8 fl oz) lukewarm milk

To finish:
beaten egg
sugar
chopped nuts
melted butter
cinnamon
currants
sultanas

1 Melt the butter and allow to cool. Place the flour in a bowl. Add the sugar and salt, mix, and make a well in the centre. In a small bowl, cream the yeast in a little of the milk and add to the flour with the butter and remaining milk. Mix with a spoon until all the milk and butter have been absorbed, then cover with a damp cloth and leave to rise in a warm place for 2 hours or until the dough has doubled in size. Meanwhile, grease three baking sheets.

2 Knock down and knead the dough until soft and smooth. Divide into three portions and shape as follows.

3 To make a Cinnamon Twist, take one portion of dough and divide it into three equal pieces. Roll each piece between floured hands into a long strand. Braid the strands together lightly, then cover and allow the twist to rise on a baking sheet for 45 minutes. Heat the oven to 180°C (350°F), Gas Mark 4. Brush with beaten egg and sprinkle with sugar and chopped nuts. Bake for 15–20 minutes.

4 To make a Cinnamon Ring, roll out the second portion of dough as thinly as possible on a floured work surface. Brush with melted butter and sprinkle heavily with sugar and cinnamon. Roll up like a Swiss roll and join the ends together to make a ring. Make sure the ends are well sealed. Place the ring on a baking sheet to rise. Cut almost through the dough at 2.5 cm (1 inch) intervals with scissors. Turn the leaves of dough thus formed to alternate sides to expose the filling. Allow to rise again for 45 minutes. Brush with beaten egg and bake at 180°C (350°F), Gas Mark 4 for 15–20 minutes. Then increase the oven temperature to 200°C (400°F), Gas Mark 6.

5 To make Fruit and Nut Buns, roll out the remaining portion of the dough as thinly as possible on a floured work surface. Brush with melted butter and sprinkle heavily with sugar, currants, sultanas and chopped nuts. Roll up like a Swiss roll and cut into 2.5 cm (1 inch) slices to form 12 small buns. Decorate each bun by cutting with scissors in different patterns. Allow to rise on a baking sheet for 45 minutes. Brush with beaten egg and bake at 200°C (400°F), Gas Mark 6 for 5–10 minutes.

Makes 2 'loaves' and 12 buns

soft fruit loaf

Preparation time: 30 minutes
Cooking time: 50–60 minutes

500 g (1 lb) cottage cheese
500 g (1 lb) plain flour
2 teaspoons baking powder
2 eggs, beaten
150 g (5 oz) caster sugar
1 tablespoon vanilla sugar
pinch of salt
1 tablespoon grated lemon rind
1 tablespoon chopped almonds
1 tablespoon raisins
2 tablespoons chopped mixed
　candied fruit
2 tablespoons chopped mixed peel

Topping:
15 g (½ oz) butter, melted
1 tablespoon icing sugar
1 tablespoon vanilla sugar

1　Grease a baking sheet with butter or margarine and sprinkle with flour. Heat the oven to 190°C (375°F), Gas Mark 5.

2　Press the cottage cheese through a sieve or grind in a blender. Sift the flour with the baking powder on to a pastry board and form a well in the centre. Add the cottage cheese, eggs, sugar, vanilla sugar, salt, lemon rind, nuts, fruit and peel. Mix to a firm dough, knead lightly, and form into a loaf. Place on a baking sheet and bake for 50–60 minutes.

3　Remove from the oven, transfer the loaf to a wire cooling rack and brush with melted butter while still hot. Mix the icing sugar and vanilla sugar and sift generously over the loaf.

Serves 12

greek festival bread

Preparation time: 30 minutes, plus rising
Cooking time: 30 minutes

1　Prepare the dough, adding the sultanas with the yeast mixture. Cover and leave to rise in a warm place until doubled in size, then knock down and leave to rise again. After the second rising, turn on to a floured work surface and knead lightly. Divide into three and roll each portion into a ball.

2　Place the balls on a large greased baking sheet in a clover leaf pattern, 1–2.5 cm (½–1 inch) apart. Cover and leave in a warm place to rise again until doubled, about 30 minutes. Bake in a heated oven at 190°C (375°F), Gas Mark 5 for about 30 minutes or until lightly browned and a skewer inserted in the centre comes out clean. Ice when cool, and decorate with glacé cherries and almonds.

Serves 8

1 quantity stollen dough, as for
　Date and Almond Stollen (see
　page 94), made without the
　almonds
175 g (6 oz) sultanas

To decorate:
glacé icing
glacé cherries
whole almonds

panettone

This sweet yeast cake is traditionally part of the Christmas fare in Italy. According to one legend it is a contraction of pane de Tonio: Tonio, a poor Milanese baker, had a pretty daughter with whom a nobleman was in love. As she could not be married without a dowry, Tonio provided all the ingredients necessary to make an excellent cake. Today it is served with coffee and for breakfast throughout the year in many regions.

Preparation time: 30 minutes, plus rising
Cooking time: 55 minutes

1 tablespoon dried yeast
5 fl oz (¼ pint) lukewarm milk
75 g (3 oz), plus 1 teaspoon caster
  sugar
500 g (1 lb) plain flour
¼ teaspoon salt
1 egg
4 egg yolks
finely grated rind of 1 orange
1 teaspoon vanilla essence
150 g (5 oz) unsalted butter,
  softened
75 g (3 oz) chopped mixed peel
150 g (5 oz) sultanas

1 Mix the yeast in a small bowl with 4 tablespoons of the milk and 1 teaspoon of the sugar. Leave for 10 minutes until frothy. Grease and line a 15 cm (6 inch) round cake tin with a double layer of greaseproof paper which extends 10 cm (4 inches) above the rim.

2 Mix 125 g (4 oz) of the flour and the remaining milk with the yeast mixture in a large bowl. Cover and leave to rise for 30 minutes.

3 Add the remaining flour, sugar, and salt, the egg, egg yolks, orange rind, vanilla essence and softened butter and mix to a dough. Turn out on to a floured surface and knead lightly until smooth and elastic. Put in a bowl, cover and leave to rise until doubled in volume.

4 Turn the dough on to a surface and work in the peel and sultanas. Shape into a ball and put in the prepared tin. Cover and leave to rise until the dough extends well above the rim. Heat the oven to 200°C (400°F), Gas Mark 6. Bake for 15 minutes, then reduce the oven temperature to 180°C (350°F), Gas Mark 4 and bake for a further 40 minutes until well risen and firm around the sides. Leave for 10 minutes then transfer to a wire rack to cool.

Serves 12

almond christmas wreath

Preparation time: 40 minutes, plus standing and rising
Cooking time: 45–50 minutes

Yeast mixture:
50 g (2 oz) plain flour
1 teaspoon sugar
1 teaspoon dried yeast
100 ml (3½ fl oz) lukewarm milk

Dough:
150 g (6 oz) plain flour
½ teaspoon salt
25 g (1 oz) margarine
2 teaspoons finely grated orange
  rind
1 egg, beaten

Filling:
50 g (2 oz) ground almonds
50 g (2 oz) caster sugar
1 large egg yolk

Icing:
125 g (4 oz) icing sugar, sieved
1 tablespoon orange juice
50 g (2 oz) red and green glacé
  cherries, chopped

1 Blend the flour, sugar, dried yeast and milk together in a bowl and leave in a warm place until frothy – about 15 minutes. Sift the flour and salt into a separate bowl and rub in the margarine. Add the orange rind and mix. Add the yeast mixture and beaten egg and mix to a dough that leaves the sides of the bowl clean.

2 Turn on to a lightly-floured surface and knead for about 10 minutes, until the dough feels smooth and elastic. Place in an oiled polythene bag or a bowl covered with a damp cloth and leave to rise until the dough has doubled in size. Meanwhile, grease and flour a baking sheet. Remove and knead lightly on a floured surface for 1 minute. Divide the dough in half. Roll each piece out to a rectangle 30 x 12 cm (12 x 5 inches).

3 Blend the almonds and caster sugar together and bind with the egg yolk to make marzipan. Divide the mixture in half. Dust the working surface with a little sieved icing sugar and roll out the marzipan into two rectangles a little smaller than the dough. Place one on top of each piece of dough. Roll up lengthways and seal the edge of the dough. Place the two rolls on a greased and floured baking sheet, form into a circle, and twist the ends together. Replace inside the polythene bag or cover with a damp cloth. Leave to rise in a warm place until doubled in size. Meanwhile, heat the oven to 190°C (375°F), Gas Mark 5.

4 Bake for 45–50 minutes or until golden. Remove from the oven and cool on a wire rack. Stir enough orange juice into the icing sugar to give a thick, flowing consistency. Spoon over the wreath and decorate with the red and green glacé cherries.

Serves 10

kerstkranz

This Dutch Christmas ring is an attractive cake for the Christmas table, especially when a decorative candle is placed in the centre of the ring, surrounded by sprigs of fir. It is a good idea to make the almond filling in advance and store it in an airtight container until required.

Preparation time: 40 minutes, plus chilling and rising
Cooking time: 20–25 minutes

1 egg, beaten, for glazing

Flaky pastry:
250 g (8 oz) plain flour
pinch of salt
75 g (3 oz) butter
75 g (3 oz) lard
1 teaspoon lemon juice
approx 250 ml (8 fl oz) cold water

Filling:
125 g (4 oz) ground almonds
125 g (4 oz) caster sugar
finely grated rind of 1 lemon
1 small egg, beaten
6 glacé cherries, halved

Decoration:
3–4 tablespoons apricot jam
1 tablespoon water
6 glacé cherries, halved
angelica leaves

Lemon glacé icing:
approx 1 tablespoon strained lemon juice
125 g (4 oz) icing sugar, sieved
yellow food colouring (optional)

1 For the pastry, sift the flour and salt into a bowl. Cream the fats together on a plate and divide into four. Rub one-quarter of the fat into the flour. Add the lemon juice to 150 ml (5 fl oz) of the water. Add sufficient liquid to the flour and fat to bind it into a soft, but not sticky, dough. Gather the dough into a ball, knead lightly and shape into a 'brick'. Roll out on a floured board into a rectangle about 1 cm (½ inch) thick, mark it across into three equal sections.

2 With a palette knife, flake the second quarter of fat evenly over the top two-thirds of the dough, leaving a narrow border round the edge. Fold the bottom third of the dough up, sealing in the air. Fold down and seal the top section. Give the dough a quarter turn, then repeat the above twice more, flaking in the third, and then the last quarter of fat. Roll out and fold the dough once or twice more until there are no fatty streaks to be seen. In hot weather, if the dough becomes sticky, it may be advisable to refrigerate it for a short time during making. Put the finished dough into a polythene bag and chill in the refrigerator for 2 hours or overnight if preferred.

3 Mix the almonds and sugar with the lemon rind. Work in sufficient egg to make a soft but not sticky paste. Knead into a ball. Grease a baking sheet.

4 Roll out the dough into a strip 10 x 52.5 cm (4 x 21 inches) and 3 mm (⅛ inch) thick. Roll the almond paste into a thin roll 47.5 cm (19 inches) long. Press the cherry halves deep into it at equal intervals. Place the almond paste roll over the pastry strip, just above centre. Fold the upper edge of the pastry down over the roll. Damp the lower edge with water, curl it up over the roll to just overlap the first pastry flap and press the edges firmly together. Place a 15 cm (6 inch) saucepan lid on a baking sheet and wrap the pastry roll around the outside to form a circle. Remove the lid. Damp one end of the pastry roll with water and insert it in the other end. Press the join firmly and neatly together. Cover and leave to rise for 15–20 minutes. Meanwhile, heat the oven to 230°C (450°F), Gas Mark 8.

5 Glaze with beaten egg and bake for 20–25 minutes or until well risen and golden. Heat the jam with the water and sieve it. Brush the pastry with it and arrange the cherry halves and angelica leaves round the ring.

6 To make the icing, stir the lemon juice into the icing sugar and mix well, adding a little water if necessary to achieve a thin pouring consistency. Add food colouring, if liked. Coat the Christmas ring with the icing while hot.

Serves 12–14

pamperato

This is an Umbrian sweet Christmas bread, the word Pamperato means 'peppered', and the mixture of honey, nuts, dried fruits and pepper brings to mind Medieval sweet breads. Pamperato is very rich: serve it in small pieces with coffee or a dessert wine.

Preparation time: 40 minutes
Cooking time: 20–25 minutes

140 g (4½ oz) raisins
2–3 tablespoons brandy
75 g (3 oz) walnuts, toasted
124 g (4 oz) almonds, toasted
40 g (1½ oz) pine nuts, toasted
100 g (3½ oz) semi-sweet
  chocolate, grated
75 g (3 oz) chopped candied
  orange or tangerine peel
2 tablespoons honey
2 tablespoons water
50 g (2 oz) redcurrant jelly
grated nutmeg
grated rind of 1 orange
¼ teaspoon sea salt
black pepper
125 g (4 oz) plain flour
apricot jam, melted
icing sugar, for sprinkling

1 Soak the raisins in the brandy and a little warm water for 30 minutes, then drain. Heat the oven to 180°C (350°F), Gas Mark 4.

2 Chop together the walnuts, almonds and pine nuts. Mix the nuts with the raisins, chocolate and candied citrus peel. Melt the honey in the water, then add to the fruit-and-nut mixture. Stir in the redcurrant jelly, nutmeg, rind, salt and 6–10 grindings of pepper. Reserve a little flour and mix the rest in, little by little, using a rubber spatula, until you have a dough that holds together.

3 Divide the dough into three balls. On a floured surface, shape each piece into a 13 cm (5½ inch) disk, incorporating the rest of the flour into the dough as you work. Place the disks on a buttered and floured baking sheet and bake for 20–25 minutes, until firm. Brush the top of each disk with melted apricot jam and bake for another 5 minutes. Let cool briefly, then sprinkle icing sugar through a sieve over the tops.

4 Store in an airtight container. Let mellow for 2–3 days before serving. Pamperato keeps for up to 1 month, improving as it ages.

Makes 3 (each Pamperato serves 4)

tyrolean fruit loaf

This fruit loaf is often made with a bread sourdough which combines with the fruit to give the loaf an excellent flavour.

Preparation time: 1 hour, plus standing and rising
Cooking time: 1 hour 10 minutes–1 hour 20 minutes

250 g (8 oz) dried pitted prunes
300 g (10 oz) dried pears
250 g (8 oz) dried figs
1 litre (2 pints) lukewarm water
125 g (4 oz) hazelnuts or pecans,
  coarsely chopped
125 g (4 oz) walnuts, coarsely
  chopped
125 g (4 oz) chopped mixed peel
125 g (4 oz) raisins
125 g (4 oz) currants
150 g (5 oz) caster sugar
1 teaspoon ground cinnamon
½ teaspoon each of allspice,
  aniseed and salt
1 tablespoon rum
2 tablespoons lemon juice
625 g (1¼ lb) bread dough
250 g (8 oz) strong plain flour

To decorate:
halved blanched almonds
1 glacé cherry

1 Steep the prunes, pears and figs in the lukewarm water in a covered bowl overnight. The next day, drain off the water and finely dice the fruit. Place the fruit, nuts and chopped mixed peel in a bowl with the raisins and currants. Stir in the sugar, flavourings, rum and lemon juice, cover the bowl, and steep for at least 1 hour. Add 150 g (5 oz) of the bread dough, together with the flour, and knead vigorously with the fruit.

2 Shape the mixture into two longish loaves and smooth the top using wetted hands. Divide the remaining dough into two halves and roll out on a floured worktop as thinly as possible. Wrap each fruit loaf in a sheet of dough, brush the edges with water, and squeeze together under the loaf. Place the loaves on a lightly greased baking sheet, cover with a cloth, and leave to rise at room temperature for 30 minutes. Meanwhile, heat the oven to 220°C (425°F), Gas Mark 7.

3 Brush the tops of the loaves with water and decorate with the almonds and glacé cherries. Bake for 10 minutes, then reduce the oven temperature to 180°C (350°F), Gas Mark 4 and bake for a further 1 hour–1 hour 10 minutes, until cooked.

Serves 15

danish pastries

The fame of these delicious pastries has travelled far and wide. They can be shaped in various ways and contain a variety of fillings such as marzipan, custard, lemon curd and fruit and nuts. In this recipe, marzipan is used – it can be homemade or shop-bought.

Preparation time: 30 minutes, plus rising
Cooking time: 15–20 minutes

250 g (8 oz) plain flour
pinch of salt
175 g (6 oz) butter
15 g (½ oz) fresh yeast
15 g (½ oz) caster sugar
5 tablespoons lukewarm water
1 egg, beaten

Marzipan:
300 g (10 oz) ground almonds
300 g (10 oz) caster sugar
2 egg yolks
2 tablespoons lemon or orange juice

Glacé icing:
1 tablespoon water
125 g (4 oz) icing sugar, sifted

1 Sift the flour and salt into a warmed mixing bowl; rub in 25 g (1 oz) of the butter. Blend the yeast with the sugar and water. Stir into the flour with the beaten egg and mix to a soft dough. Turn on to a floured board and knead lightly for about 5 minutes until smooth. Put in an oiled polythene bag and refrigerate for 10 minutes.

2 Cream the remaining butter with a spatula. Roll out the dough into a rectangle 1 cm (½ inch) thick. Spread the butter evenly over one-half of the dough, leaving a 2.5 cm (1 inch) border all around the edge. Fold over the other half of the dough, seal the edges with a rolling pin, and give the pastry a quarter-turn. Re-roll, fold, seal, and quarter-turn. Repeat three times, chilling for 10 minutes between each rolling. Put in the polythene bag and chill for at least 30 minutes before shaping.

3 Roll out the dough and divide in half. Roll one half into a 30 x 20 cm (12 x 8 inch) rectangle. Cut into six 10 cm (4 inch) squares.

4 Make the marzipan by sifting the almonds and sugar in a mixing bowl. Beat the egg yolks with the fruit juice and stir into the dry ingredients. Work into a stiff paste and knead until smooth. If the paste is sticky, work in a little more sugar; if dry and crumbly, add a little more juice.

5 Divide the marzipan into fourteen pieces, roll six into little balls and flatten slightly. Place one in the centre of each square and brush with beaten egg. Draw up the corners together in the centre like an envelope and seal with beaten egg. Place the pastries on a greased baking sheet, cover, and leave in a warm place for about 20 minutes until puffy.

6 Roll the remaining dough into a 25 cm (10 inch) square and divide into quarters. Cut each of the squares diagonally making eight triangles. Roll the remaining pieces of marzipan into tiny cylinders. Place in the centre of the long side of each triangle. Brush the pastry edges with beaten egg and roll up with the point underneath. Curve into a crescent shape. Place on a greased baking sheet, cover and leave in a warm place for 20 minutes until puffy.

7 Heat the oven to 220°C (425°F), Gas Mark 7. Bake the pastries for 15–20 minutes or until crisp and golden. To make the glacé icing stir the water into the icing sugar very gradually and mix to a spreading consistency, adding a little more water if necessary. Brush the pastries with the glacé icing and cool on a wire rack.

Makes 14

pandolce

An Italian candied fruit and nut bread. Pandolce can be frozen for up to 6 months. Thaw at room temperature for 4 hours or bake at 150°C (300°F), Gas Mark 2 for about 40 minutes.

Preparation time: 25 minutes, plus standing and rising
Cooking time: about 1 hour

2 teaspoons fresh yeast
125 g (4 oz) caster sugar
4 tablespoons lukewarm water
500 g (1 lb) plain flour
75 g (3 oz) butter, melted
1 egg, beaten
250 g (8 oz) crystallised fruits,
   chopped or chopped mixed peel
75 g (3 oz) blanched almonds,
   chopped

1 Crumble the yeast into a small bowl. Cream with 1 teaspoon of the sugar, and mix in the warm water. Leave in a warm place to froth – about 10 minutes.

2 Sift the flour into a bowl and make a well in the centre; add the yeast liquid, the remaining sugar, the melted butter and the beaten egg. Work to a smooth dough. Put the dough into a floured bowl and cover with a damp kitchen towel or large freezer bag. Leave in a warm place for 1 hour or until doubled in size. Meanwhile, grease a baking sheet or 18 cm (7 inch) brioche tin.

3 Knock back the dough and knead in the chopped fruits and almonds. Shape the dough into a large round loaf and place on the baking sheet or brioche tin. Cover again and leave for 40–45 minutes or until doubled in size. Heat the oven to 220°C (425°F), Gas Mark 7.

4 Bake in the preheated oven for 50–55 minutes, covering with aluminium foil once the top has browned well. Test with a thin skewer to see that the bread is cooked through; if the skewer does not come out clean, bake the bread for 10 minutes longer. Cool on a wire rack.

Serves 12–15

gugelhopf

This is the yeast cake of Alsace from which babas and savarins were developed. Gugelhopf is studded with rum-soaked currants and is cooked in a distinctive fluted ring mould. In Alsace, Gugelhopf is eaten on Sunday for breakfast, and is traditionally prepared the night before.

Preparation time: 30 minutes, plus rising
Cooking time: 50 minutes–1 hour

butter, for greasing
40 g (1½ oz) slivered almonds
75 g (3 oz) currants
75 g (3 oz) raisins
3 tablespoons rum
175 ml (6 fl oz) milk
25 g (1 oz) fresh yeast
375 g (12 oz) flour
pinch of salt
1½ tablespoons caster sugar
3 eggs, lightly beaten
125 g (4 oz) butter, melted and
  slightly cooled
icing sugar, sifted, for dusting

1 Generously butter a 20 cm (8 inch) gugelhopf tin or bundt tin and press slivered almonds into the butter. Refrigerate until needed.

2 Soak the currants and raisins in the rum. Warm the milk to blood heat, pour on to the yeast, and stir until dissolved. Sift the flour and salt into a warm bowl. Make a well in the centre and add the milk mixture, sugar, eggs and melted butter. Beat well and add the soaked fruits. Pour the well-mixed batter into the prepared tin, which should be three-quarters full. Cover with a damp cloth and stand in a warm place for 20–30 minutes or until the mixture has risen to 2.5 cm (1 inch) below the top of the mould. Heat the oven to 190°C (375°F), Gas Mark 5.

3 Bake for 50 minutes–1 hour or until a fine skewer inserted in the centre comes out clean. Stand for a few minutes, then unmould on to a wire rack to cool. Dust with icing sugar.

Serves 10

piped choux rings

Preparation time: 50 minutes
Cooking time: 10 minutes

oil, for deep-frying

Choux paste:
250 ml (8 fl oz) water
50 g (2 oz) butter
pinch of salt
150 g (5 oz) plain flour, sifted
4 eggs

Icing:
150 g (5 oz) icing sugar, sifted
2 tablespoons rum
1 tablespoon water

1 Cut a sheet of greaseproof paper to fit into a deep-fryer and brush with oil.

2 Heat the water gently with the butter and salt until the butter is melted, then bring to the boil. Add the sifted flour all at once, remove from the heat, and stir until the dough comes away from the sides of the pan and forms a ball.

3 Return to the heat and cook for 1 minute stirring continuously. Place in a bowl, leave to cool slightly, then stir in the beaten eggs one after the other.

4 Heat the oil to 180°C (350°F) in the deep-fryer. Place the choux paste in a piping bag fitted with a large star nozzle and pipe rings on to the greaseproof paper: the rings should not be too large. Place the paper with the rings attached into the hot oil in the pan, with the rings under the paper. Remove the paper when the rings become free of it. Fry the rings on both sides until golden then drain on kitchen paper. Repeat until all the rings are cooked.

5 Blend the icing sugar with the rum and water, and thinly ice the choux rings.

Makes 20

prianiki with honey

Preparation time: 20 minutes
Cooking time: 20 minutes

1 Prepare moulds such as star, bell or fir tree shapes by buttering generously and dusting with flour. Heat the oven to 230°C (450°F), Gas Mark 8.

2 Warm the honey over a gentle heat in a large saucepan. Whisk it by hand or with an electric whisk, then remove from the heat and stir in the flour, egg yolks, almonds and lemon rind.

4 In a clean, dry bowl, whisk the egg whites to stiff peaks. Fold them into the honey mixture with a little grated nutmeg. Pour into the prepared moulds.

4 Bake for 5 minutes, then reduce the oven temperature to 190°C (375°F), Gas Mark 5, and bake for a further 10–15 minutes. Cool the prianiki for 10 minutes in the moulds before turning on to wire racks to cool completely.

Serves 10

butter, for greasing
1 kg (2 lb) clear honey
1.075 kg (2 lb 3 oz) plain flour
4 eggs, separated
5 bitter almonds, ground
grated rind of ½ lemon
nutmeg, grated, to taste

pistachio nut stollen

It is customary to make two stollen at a time, one for the household and one to give away to friends and family.

Preparation time: 40 minutes, plus rising
Cooking time: 50 minutes–1 hour

625 g (1¼ lb) strong plain flour
25 g (1 oz) fresh yeast
300 ml (½ pint) lukewarm milk
1 egg
75 g (3 oz) caster sugar
½ teaspoon salt
grated rind of ½ lemon
1 teaspoon vanilla essence
175 g (6 oz) butter
175 g (6 oz) chopped mixed peel
125 g (4 oz) pistachio nuts
50 g (2 oz) icing sugar
1 tablespoon maraschino liqueur
125 g (4 oz) marzipan
65 g (2½ oz) melted butter, for
  coating
125 g (4 oz) icing sugar, for
  sprinkling

1 Make a smooth, firm dough, using the method described for Austrian Stollen (see page 115), using 500 g (1 lb) of the flour, the yeast, milk, egg, sugar, salt, lemon rind and vanilla. Cover the bowl and leave to rise for 10 minutes.

2 Meanwhile, work the butter together with the remaining flour and the chopped mixed peel. Work this mixture into the dough and leave to rise for a further 30 minutes. Line a baking sheet with greased greaseproof paper.

3 Work the pistachio nuts, icing sugar and maraschino into the marzipan. Roll this marzipan to about 1 cm (½ inch) thick and cut into 1 cm (½ inch) cubes. Work these quickly into the yeast dough so that they remain whole.

4 Shape the dough to make two stollen and place on the baking sheet. Cover with oiled clingfilm and leave to rise for 20–25 minutes. Meanwhile, heat the oven to 200°C (400°F), Gas Mark 6.

5 Bake for 50 minutes–1 hour. Brush the melted butter all over the warm stollen and then sprinkle with the icing sugar.

Serves 15

grittibanz

This is the Swiss version of the Saint Nicholas Loaf, a figurative loaf that is baked in many parts of Germany and Austria to celebrate Saint Nicholas' Day. These are simple figures whose only form of decoration are two currants pressed into the dough for eyes. The body is made from a ball of dough which is rolled into a long oval before the legs are made by cutting from the base up to the centre with a knife. The sides are then cut to make the arms. The Swiss Grittibanz, which were known as 'Chriddibenz' when they first appeared in 1850, are quite intricate fabrications, regardless of whether they come from the bakery or are made at home.

Preparation time: 30 minutes, plus rising
Cooking time: 20–35 minutes

1 kg (2 lb) strong plain flour
40 g (1½ oz) fresh yeast, crumbled
450 ml (¾ pint) lukewarm milk
125 g (4 oz) butter
125 g (4 oz) caster sugar
1 teaspoon salt
grated rind of 1 lemon
2 eggs
2 egg yolks and water, for glazing

1 Sift the flour into a bowl, make a well in the centre, and stir the crumbled yeast into the well with the lukewarm milk and leave for 10 minutes or until frothy. Sprinkle this mixture with flour, cover the bowl, and leave to stand until the flour shows distinct cracks.

2 Meanwhile melt the butter and beat with the sugar, salt, lemon rind and eggs. Add this to the yeast mixture and work all the ingredients together to make a uniform dough. The dough should be neither too firm nor too soft so that it can be shaped easily. Cover with oiled clingfilm and leave to rise for 1–1½ hours. Grease one or two baking sheets.

3 The figures (two to four from the quantities given) are formed from a flattened ball of dough. The arms, legs, head and hat are shaped from the ball and glazed with egg yolk, then other elements such as beard, nose and eyes are shaped separately and stuck on with egg yolk. Leave the finished figures to rise for at least 20–25 minutes. Heat the oven to 190°C (375°F), Gas Mark 5.

4 Bake the figures for 20–35 minutes depending on their size.

Makes 2–4

austrian stollen

Preparation time: 40 minutes, plus rising
Cooking time: 1 hour

625 g (1¼ lb) strong plain flour
25 g (1 oz) fresh yeast
300 ml (½ pint) lukewarm milk
50 g (2 oz) caster sugar
1 egg
1 teaspoon vanilla essence
grated rind of ½ lemon
½ teaspoon salt
250 g (8 oz) butter
140 g (4½ oz) raisins
4 tablespoons blanched almonds,
  chopped
75 g (3oz) chopped mixed peel
1 tablespoon rum
65 g (2½ oz) melted butter, for
  coating
125 g (4 oz) icing sugar, for
  sprinkling

1   Sift 500 g (1lb) of the flour into a bowl, make a well, and stir the crumbled fresh yeast into the well with the lukewarm milk. Sprinkle the mixture with flour, cover the bowl, and leave for 20 minutes.

2   Add the sugar, egg, vanilla essence, lemon rind and salt to the yeast mixture and knead to give a dry, firm dough. Leave the dough to rise for 30 minutes. Work the butter with the remaining flour, work into the yeast dough, and then leave the dough to rise for a further 30 minutes.

3   Mix together the raisins, almonds and chopped mixed peel and steep in the rum. Then work the fruit mixture quickly into the dough and leave to rise for a further 30 minutes. Knead gently on a lightly floured board. Cover a baking sheet with greased greaseproof paper.

4   Shape the dough into two balls and roll these into long loaves of about 30 cm (12 inches) in length. Roll the centres of the loaves with the rolling pin so that they are thicker down both sides. Round off the ends and then fold over lengthways into the familiar stollen shape. Place the stollen on the baking sheet, cover with oiled clingfilm, and leave to rise for 20–30 minutes or until visibly increased in volume. Meanwhile, heat the oven to 200°C (400°F), Gas Mark 6.

5   Bake for about 1 hour and test with a skewer to make sure that each stollen is cooked through. While still warm, brush all over with the melted butter and sprinkle with the icing sugar. This butter-and-sugar coating will keep the stollen moist.

Serves 15

desserts

chestnut ice cream

This ice cream can be served simply scooped into individual dishes or moulded and decorated for an impressive dessert. For the latter, freeze the ice cream in a 1 kg (2 lb) loaf tin lined with aluminium foil. To serve, unmould and decorate with piped whipped cream and chocolate curls.

Preparation time: 40 minutes, plus freezing
Cooking time: 15 minutes

**475 g (15 oz) can unsweetened
  chestnut purée**
4 tablespoons brandy
175 g (6 oz) caster sugar
450 ml (¾ pint) double cream
2 egg whites
**chocolate curls, to decorate
  (optional)**

Chocolate sauce:
**175 g (6 oz) plain chocolate, broken
  into pieces**
150 ml (¼ pint) water
125 g (4 oz) caster sugar

1 Put the chestnut purée, brandy and 50 g (2 oz) of the sugar in a bowl and beat well until smooth. Whip the cream until it will stand in soft peaks, then fold into the chestnut purée.

2 Whisk the egg whites until stiff, then gradually whisk in the remaining sugar. Continue whisking until the mixture is very stiff. Fold into the chestnut mixture, then turn into a rigid container and freeze.

3 To make the chocolate sauce, put all the ingredients in a saucepan and heat very gently until the chocolate has melted and the sugar dissolved. Simmer, uncovered, for 10 minutes, then remove from the heat and leave to cool.

4 Transfer the ice cream to the refrigerator 20 minutes before serving to soften. Scoop into individual dishes, pour over the sauce and decorate with chocolate curls, if desired. The sauce can also be made in advance and frozen for up to 3 months.

Serves 8

english raspberry trifle

Preparation time: about 40 minutes, plus chilling
Cooking time: about 5 minutes

20 cm (8 inch) sponge cake or
  6–8 trifle sponges
3 tablespoons raspberry jam
4 tablespoons sherry
250–375 g (8–12 oz) frozen
  raspberries, partly defrosted

Custard:
2 tablespoons cornflour
600 ml (1 pint) milk
4 egg yolks
4 tablespoons caster sugar
few drops of vanilla essence

Topping:
300 ml (½ pint) double cream or
  whipping cream
walnut halves
angelica

1 Split the cake in half and sandwich together with the jam or, if using trifle sponges, spread these with the jam. Cut the sponge into 2.5 cm (1 inch) cubes and place in a glass serving bowl. Sprinkle with the sherry.

2 Arrange the raspberries over the sponge and leave until almost completely defrosted, so that the juices run down into the sponge.

3 To make the custard, blend the cornflour with the milk in a bowl, then whisk in the egg yolks and strain into a saucepan. Add the sugar and bring slowly to the boil, stirring continuously. Cook until thickened, stirring, then remove from the heat and stir in the vanilla essence. Allow the custard to cool slightly, then pour over the raspberries and chill in the refrigerator until set.

4 Whip the cream until stiff and put into a piping bag fitted with a large star nozzle. Pipe a lattice or wheel design on top of the trifle. Decorate with walnuts and angelica and chill again in the refrigerator before serving.

Serves 10–12

cassata gelata

Meaning 'in a case or chest', cassata is the name of two famous Italian desserts. As the name suggests, both were traditionally made in the form of a case with a filling, but nowadays they are often made in layers.

Preparation time: 30 minutes

500 g (1 lb) mixed candied fruit
125 g (4 oz) sugared almonds
1 litre (1¾ pint) carton ice cream,
  softened
475 ml (16 fl oz) double cream,
  whipped and sweetened with
  2 tablespoons caster sugar

1 Chop the candied fruit and sugared almonds. Line a pudding basin with softened ice cream. Fill the centre with the lightly sweetened whipped cream mixed with the chopped fruit and almonds. (If preferred, the ice cream and whipped cream mixture can be arranged in layers.) Freeze until firm.

2 Dip the outside of the mould briefly in hot water and turn out on to a plate.

Serves 12

traditional english christmas pudding

A pudding traditionally served at Christmas in Britain. The pudding was originally made like a large ball as in this recipe. Christmas pudding improves with keeping as it allows the mixture to mature. If possible, make it 3–4 months before Christmas.

Preparation time: 20 minutes
Cooking time: 8–8½ hours

175 g (6 oz) plain flour
2 teaspoons ground mixed spice
1 teaspoon ground cinnamon
½ teaspoon grated nutmeg
175 g (6 oz) fresh white
  breadcrumbs
175 g (6 oz) butter
175 g (6 oz) soft brown sugar
375 g (12 oz) sultanas
250 g (8 oz) raisins
250 g (8 oz) currants
75 g (3 oz) chopped mixed peel
grated rind and juice of 1 orange
2 eggs, beaten
125 ml (4 fl oz) brown ale

1 Sift the flour and spices into a bowl, add the breadcrumbs, then rub in the butter. Stir in the sugar, add the remaining ingredients, and mix thoroughly.

2 Turn into a greased 1.8 litre (3-pint) pudding basin, cover with cheesecloth or greaseproof paper and aluminium foil, and steam for 6 hours, topping up the saucepan with boiling water as necessary.

3 Cool slightly, then remove the cloth or paper, and leave to cool completely. Cover with clean greaseproof paper and aluminium foil, and store in a cool, dry place.

4 To serve, steam the pudding again for 2–2½ hours. Unmould on to a warmed serving dish. If liked, pour over 2–3 tablespoons warmed brandy and ignite. Top with a sprig of holly and serve with cream or Brandy Butter (see below).

Serves 8–10

brandy butter

Preparation time: 5 minutes

175 g (6 oz) unsalted butter
175 g (6 oz) caster sugar
3–4 tablespoons brandy

1 Cream the butter until soft then gradually add the sugar and brandy, beating thoroughly with each addition.

2 Pile into a serving dish. Chill until firm.

Serves 8–10

french christmas pudding

Chestnuts are a versatile food suitable for use in savoury dressings, soups and pies, as well as a basis for sweet flans and puddings. Their flavour is enhanced by chocolate.

Preparation time: 30 minutes
Cooking time: 2 hours

475 g (15 oz) can chestnut purée
125 g (4 oz) unsalted butter,
  softened
4 eggs, separated
175 g (6 oz) caster sugar
2 tablespoons brandy (optional)
4 marrons glacés, sliced, to
  decorate (optional)

Chocolate sauce:
150 ml (¼ pint) double cream
250 g (8 oz) plain chocolate, broken
  into pieces
2 tablespoons brandy

1 Heat the oven to 180°C (350°F), Gas Mark 4. Grease and line a 1 litre (1¾ pint) enamel loaf tin.

2 Cream the chestnut purée and butter, then beat in the egg yolks, sugar and brandy, if using. Whisk the egg whites until stiff and fold them into the chestnut mixture, then pour into the prepared tin. Place the tin in a water-bath and bake for 2 hours, until set. Cover with a piece of buttered aluminium foil if necessary during cooking.

3 Meanwhile, prepare the sauce. Heat the cream in a small heavy-based saucepan over a gentle heat; do not let it boil. Add the chocolate and brandy. Stir over a very gentle heat until the chocolate has melted and the sauce is smooth.

4 Remove the pudding from the oven and cool in the tin for 5–10 minutes. Loosen it with a knife and unmould on to a warmed platter. Coat with a little chocolate sauce and decorate with the marrons glacés, if using. Serve the remaining sauce separately.

Serves 8

ao 'a' tea roa

Preparation time: 30 minutes, plus standing
Cooking time: 2 hours

250 g (8 oz) plain flour
250 g (8 oz) soft brown sugar
175 g (6 oz) raisins
50 g (2 oz) chopped mixed peel
grated rind of 1 lemon
½ teaspoon mixed spice
125 g (4 oz) butter, softened
2 teaspoons bicarbonate of soda
350 ml (12 fl oz) boiling water
2 eggs, beaten

Long white cloud topping:
475 g (15 oz) can apricot halves
¼ teaspoon ground cinnamon
1 litre (1¾ pint) carton vanilla ice
  cream
2–3 tablespoons brandy

1 Sift the flour into a bowl, add the sugar, raisins, peel, lemon rind and spice and mix well. Cut the butter into small pieces and dot over the mixture.

2 Dissolve the bicarbonate of soda in the boiling water and pour over the mixture. Mix lightly, cover with a clean kitchen towel and leave to stand overnight.

3 The next day, add the beaten eggs and turn into a greased 1.8 litre (3 pint) mould. Cover with cheesecloth or greaseproof paper (leaving some room for expansion) and tie securely with string. Put the basin into a saucepan of boiling water, so that the water comes halfway up the basin and simmer for at least 2 hours, topping up the water as necessary.

4 Line a freezer tray or other container measuring 25 x 10 cm (10 x 4 inches) with a double lining of aluminium foil. Remove the warm Christmas pudding from the bowl and pack it into the tray. Chill until required.

5 Purée the apricots with the cinnamon. To serve the pudding, unmould it on to a serving platter. Put slices or scoops of ice cream on top of the pudding and coat with the apricot mixture. Bring to the table, pour warmed brandy around the dish and set it alight. Serve at once.

nesselrode pudding

Preparation time: 20 minutes, plus chilling

3 egg yolks
175 g (6 oz) sugar
1 tablespoon gelatine, softened in
  2 tablespoons cold water
600 ml (1 pint) single cream
75 g (3 oz) canned crushed
  pineapple, drained
75 g (3 oz) raisins
2 tablespoons glacé cherries,
  soaked in 2 tablespoons rum
40 g (1½ oz) dark chocolate,
  chopped, plus extra, grated, for
  decorating

1 Beat the egg yolks and sugar until light and frothy. Add the softened gelatine to the cream. Beat the egg yolk mixture into the cream and chill until the mixture is almost set (about 1 hour). Beat in the pineapple, raisins, cherries and chopped chocolate. Pour into a mould and freeze until set. When set, decorate with the grated chocolate.

Serves 15

bombe noël

A rich vanilla ice cream mixed with candied fruits and nuts soaked in brandy. Rich but cooling, a great idea for Christmas in the south and southwest of France.

Preparation time: 20 minutes, plus freezing
Cooking time: 10 minutes

125 g (4 oz) glacé cherries, chopped

50 g (2 oz) angelica, chopped

50 g (2 oz) crystallised pineapple, chopped

50 g (2 oz) preserved ginger, drained and chopped

75 g (3 oz) seedless raisins

4 tablespoons brandy

3 egg yolks

75 g (3 oz) caster sugar

300 ml (½ pint) single cream

150 ml (¼ pint) double cream, plus 6 extra tablespoons, whipped, to serve

6 tablespoons toasted chopped almonds

crystallised ginger, to decorate

1 Put the chopped cherries, angelica, pineapple, ginger and raisins in a bowl. Pour the brandy over them and leave to macerate for 1 hour.

2 Put the egg yolks and caster sugar in a bowl and beat until thoroughly blended. Bring the single cream just to the boil in a saucepan, remove from the heat, and stir gradually into the yolk mixture. Transfer to the top of a double boiler or a heatproof bowl over a pan of simmering water and cook gently, stirring constantly, until the custard is thick enough to coat the back of a spoon. Strain into a bowl and leave to cool, stirring occasionally to prevent a skin forming.

3 Whip the double cream until it stands in soft peaks, then fold in the cold custard. Pour into a rigid container, cover and freeze for 2–3 hours until half-frozen. Remove from the freezer and stir in the macerated fruits with the brandy and the almonds. Spoon into a 1 litre (1¾ pint) aluminium foil pudding bowl and level the surface.

4 To freeze, cover the bowl with aluminium foil, then wrap in a polythene bag. Seal, label, and freeze for up to 3 months.

5 To thaw and serve, unwrap the bowl and invert on to a serving plate. Rub with a cloth wrung out in very hot water until the bombe drops out. Place in the refrigerator for 30 minutes, before serving decorated with crystallised ginger, if liked.

Serves 6–8

mincemeat meringue pie

Preparation time: 30 minutes, plus chilling
Cooking time: 30 minutes

Pastry:

175 g (6 oz) plain flour
2 tablespoons caster sugar
½ teaspoon salt
75 g (3 oz) butter or margarine
1 egg yolk
2 tablespoons iced water

Filling:

6 apples
50 g (2 oz) butter
125 g (4 oz) brown sugar
finely grated rind and juice of
** 1 lemon**
375 g (12 oz) mincemeat

Topping:

3 egg whites
½ teaspoon cream of tartar
6 tablespoons icing sugar

1 Stir the flour, sugar and salt in a bowl. Cut in the butter or margarine, until the mixture resembles coarse breadcrumbs. Combine the egg yolk and iced water and sprinkle over the crumbs, tossing with a fork until the mixture binds together. Shape into a ball, wrap in clingfilm, and refrigerate for 30 minutes. Meanwhile, heat the oven to 190°C (375°F), Gas Mark 5.

2 Roll out the dough on a lightly floured board and use to line a 23 cm (9 inch) loose-bottomed quiche dish or pie tin. Prick the bottom of the crust with a fork and refrigerate for 30 minutes. Line the crust with aluminium foil and dried beans and bake for 15 minutes. Remove the foil and beans, return to the oven, and bake for 5 minutes longer or until the pastry is golden. Cool on a wire rack. Increase the oven temperature to 200°C (400°F), Gas Mark 6.

3 Meanwhile, peel, core and slice the apples into rings. Melt the butter in a saucepan, add the apple rings, brown sugar, lemon rind and juice, and cook over a low heat for a few minutes until the apples are coated. Cool.

4 Arrange half the apple rings in the bottom of the cooled crust. Spoon the mincemeat over the apples and top with the remaining apple rings. Beat the egg whites with the cream of tartar until foaming, then beat in the icing sugar, 1 tablespoon at a time. Beat until stiff peaks form. Pipe the meringue over the tart, covering the filling completely. Bake for 8–10 minutes or until lightly browned. Remove from the oven and let cool.

Serves 8–10

christmas kasha

Kasha is a traditional Christmas Eve dessert from Russia.

Preparation time: 20 minutes, plus standing
Cooking time: 3 hours

1 Put the semolina in a sieve and rinse them, then simmer over a very low heat for several hours, until they swell and become soft, but not sticky. Drain and return the semolina to a clean saucepan.

2 In a measuring jug, mix the honey with the boiling water. Stir well, then add to the semolina. Bring the mixture to the boil, then leave to cool.

3 Put the raisins in a small bowl with the rum, and the apricots in a separate bowl with the water. Leave to stand until plump, then add the dried fruits to the semolina mixture with the walnuts. Stir well, then leave in a cool place for several hours.

Serves 6

350 g (12 oz) coarse semolina
425 g (14 oz) honey
250 ml (8 fl oz) boiling water
125 g (4 oz) raisins
5 tablespoons rum
125 g (4 oz) dried apricots
300 ml (½ pint) water
125 g (4 oz) walnuts

monte bianco

Preparation time: 20 minutes
Cooking time: 15 minutes

50 g (2 oz) sugar
5 tablespoons milk
475 g (15 oz) can unsweetened
   chestnut purée
250 ml (8 fl oz) double cream
1 tablespoon rum
grated chocolate, to decorate

1 Dissolve the sugar in the milk over a gentle heat. Add the chestnut purée and stir until smooth. Cool, then chill.

2 Whip the cream and fold half into the chestnut mixture with the rum. Fill a greaseproof paper funnel with the chestnut cream and pipe so that it falls loosely into a cone shape on six individual serving dishes. Top with the remaining cream and sprinkle with grated chocolate.

Serves 6

zuccotto

Zuccotto has a traditional decoration of icing sugar and cocoa powder striped like a beach ball. If you want to make the traditional decoration cut a circle of greaseproof paper to cover the zuccotto, fold it into eight sections, then cut out alternate sections. Position the paper over the zuccotto and sift cocoa powder over. Move the paper round to cover the cocoa powder and sift icing sugar over.

Preparation time: 15–20 minutes, plus chilling
Cooking time: 35–40 minutes

3 large eggs
75 g (3 oz) caster sugar
50 g (2 oz) plain flour
1 tablespoon cocoa powder, plus
  extra for dusting
1 tablespoon oil

Filling:
4 tablespoons brandy
350 ml (12 fl oz) double cream
40 g (1½ oz) icing sugar, sifted
50 g (2 oz) plain chocolate,
  chopped
25 g (1 oz) almonds, chopped and
  toasted
175 g (6 oz) cherries, pitted
2 tablespoons Kirsch

1 Heat the oven to 180°C (350°F), Gas Mark 4. Grease a 20 cm (8 inch) cake tin.

2 Place the eggs and caster sugar in a bowl and whisk over a saucepan of hot water until thick. Sift the flour and cocoa powder into the bowl and fold in, then fold in the oil. Spoon into the cake tin and bake for 35–40 minutes. Turn on to a wire rack.

3 When cool, cut the sponge in half horizontally and line a 1.8 litre (3 pint) bowl with one layer. Sprinkle with brandy. Whip the cream to soft peaks. Fold in 25 g (1 oz) of the icing sugar, the chocolate, almonds, cherries and Kirsch. Spoon into the bowl and top with the remaining sponge. Cover with a plate and chill.

4 Turn out on to a plate, sprinkle with the remaining icing sugar and cocoa powder to make a pattern.

Serves 6–8

cassata alla siciliana

This dessert may be prepared up to 1 day in advance. Cover and chill until the point of serving. It is eaten at Christmas, Easter and at weddings.

Preparation time: 1 hour, plus chilling

500 g (1 lb) madeira cake, cut into
  1 cm (½ inch) slices
4 tablespoons maraschino or
  kirsch liqueur
500 g (1 lb) fresh ricotta cheese,
  drained and sieved
150 ml (¼ pint) single cream
50 g (2 oz) sugar
1 teaspoon ground cinnamon
125 g (4 oz) dark dessert
  chocolate, finely chopped
250 g (8 oz) whole mixed
  crystallised fruits, finely chopped
25 g (1 oz) pistachio nuts,
  blanched, peeled and chopped
½ teaspoon orange-flower water
icing sugar, sifted, for dusting

1 Line the base and sides of a 1.8 litre (3 pint) charlotte mould or 18 cm (7 inch) deep cake tin with nonstick baking paper.

2 Use three-quarters of the cake slices to line the base and sides of the container, cutting and trimming them to a triangular shape to fit the mould when placed in a circle. Sprinkle 2 tablespoons of the liqueur over the cake.

3 Whip the ricotta cheese until it is creamy then beat in the cream, sugar, cinnamon, chocolate, chopped crystallised fruits and pistachio nuts. Stir in the orange-flower water. Pour this mixture into the prepared mould and smooth the top. Trim the remaining cake slices and arrange them on top. Sprinkle with the remaining liqueur. Cover and chill for 3–4 hours.

4 Carefully unmould the cake on to a serving platter and sprinkle with sifted icing sugar.

Serves 8

tarts & pies

spiced apple pie

Place the utensils – rolling pin, board, cutting utensils – in the refrigerator or freezer for a short time before making pastry. The cooler the conditions, the better the finished pastry will be.

Preparation time: 20 minutes
Cooking time: 30–40 minutes

750 g (1½ lb) cooking apples,
   peeled, cored and thinly sliced
75 g (3 oz) soft brown sugar
1 teaspoon mixed spice
4 whole cloves
caster sugar, for sprinkling

Pastry:
175 g (6 oz) plain flour
75 g (3 oz) butter or margarine
1–2 tablespoons iced water

Vanilla cream:
2 egg yolks
1 teaspoon cornflour
25 g (1 oz) caster sugar
300 ml (½ pint) milk
½ teaspoon vanilla essence

1 Heat the oven to 200°C (400°F), Gas Mark 6. Layer the apples with the sugar and spices in a 1 litre (1¾ pint) pie dish.

2 For the pastry, sift the flour into a mixing bowl; rub in the butter with your fingertips until the mixture resembles fine breadcrumbs, then add enough iced water to form a soft dough. Roll it out to a circle about 5 cm (2 inches) larger than the pie dish. Cut off a strip all round and use to cover the dampened rim of the dish; brush with water. Place the pastry circle on top and press to seal the edges. Trim and flute the edges; make a hole in the centre. Brush with water, sprinkle with sugar and bake for 30–40 minutes.

3 To make the vanilla cream, cream the egg yolks with the cornflour and sugar. Bring the milk to the boil, pour on to the egg yolk mixture, and stir well. Return to the saucepan and heat gently, stirring until the mixture is thick. Add the vanilla essence, then strain. Serve hot or cold with the pie.

Serves 4–6

star mince pie

Mincemeat is a spicy preserve consisting of a mixture of dried fruits and spices steeped in rum, brandy or other spirits. Sweet mince pies are part of the traditional Christmas fare in Britain.

Preparation time: 20 minutes, plus chilling
Cooking time: 30–40 minutes

350 g (12 oz) plain flour
175 g (6 oz) butter or margarine
75 g (3 oz) caster sugar
2 egg yolks
few drops of vanilla essence
500 g (1 lb) mincemeat

To decorate:
sifted icing sugar
glacé cherries
angelica

1 To make the sweet pastry, sift the plain flour into a mixing bowl and add the butter or margarine, caster sugar and egg yolks mixed with a few drops of vanilla essence. Combine the ingredients to form a soft dough. Cover and chill. Preheat the oven to 190°C (375°F), Gas Mark 5.

2 Roll out half the dough and line a (20 cm) 8 inch fluted flan ring or pie dish. Fill with mincemeat. Roll out the remaining dough and cut a large star-shape from the centre. Lift the pastry carefully over the filling. Seal the edges and neaten them. Bake in the centre of the oven for 30–40 minutes or until golden. Decorate with sifted icing sugar, glacé cherries and small leaves of angelica. Serve hot or cold.

Serves 6–8

black bun

Famous throughout Scotland since the 18th century, Black Bun was often made at Christmas, when it was sometimes called Yule Cake. The filling is much like a Christmas cake, but the delicate envelope of pastry gives it a special character. It requires neither eggs nor sugar.

Preparation time: 30 minutes, plus cooling
Cooking time: 2½ hours

Dough:

500 g (1 lb) plain flour
¼ teaspoon salt
250 g (8 oz) butter
1–2 tablespoons iced water

Filling:

375 g (12 oz) self-raising flour
1 teaspoon cinnamon
¼ teaspoon black pepper
¼ teaspoon grated nutmeg
500 g (1 lb) seedless raisins
500 g (1 lb) currants
50 g (2 oz) chopped mixed peel
  (optional)
50 g (2 oz) glacé cherries, chopped
125 g (4 oz) blanched almonds,
  coarsely chopped
2 tablespoons whisky
milk, for mixing
2 egg yolks, beaten

1   Heat the oven to 180°C (350°F), Gas Mark 4. Grease either a 25 x 12 cm (10 x 5 inch) bread tin or a loose-bottomed 20 cm (8 inch) cake tin.

2   Mix the flour and salt together and rub in the butter until you have a crumb-like consistency. Mix in 1 tablespoon of iced water. If the dough is still crumbly, add another tablespoon of iced water, and stir and mix until it will come away from the bowl in one piece, leaving the bowl clean.

3   Flour a board and roll the dough out to a little less than 5 mm (¼ inch) thickness. Line the bread or cake tin, moulding the dough against the sides and making sure there are no holes. Set aside a piece for the lid.

4   Mix all the dry ingredients for the filling together and then add all the fruit and the almonds. Stir well together. Stir in the whisky then add enough milk to bring it to a stiff consistency.

5   Fill the tin and smooth off flat at the top. Roll out the dough lid and lay it on loosely so that the inside can rise a little. Thrust a long skewer through the lid and filling, right to the bottom, in about eight places. Lightly prick the lid all over with a fork. Brush over with the beaten egg yolks.

6   Put the tin in the oven and bake for 2½ hours. Allow the bun to stand in the tin on a wire rack for 30 minutes before turning out.

Serves 10–12

linzertorte

This is an Austrian pastry that takes its name from the town of Linz. It is distinguished by its unique pastry made with ground nuts. Lattice biscuit cutters are available to make dough lattice easy: simply roll out the dough and run the lattice cutter over it.

Preparation time: 25 minutes
Cooking time: 25–30 minutes

150 g (6 oz) plain flour
½ teaspoon ground cinnamon
75 g (3 oz) butter
50 g (2 oz) sugar
50 g (2 oz) ground almonds
2 teaspoons finely grated lemon
  rind
2 large egg yolks
about 1 tablespoon lemon juice
325 g (11 oz) raspberry jam

1 Heat the oven to 190°C (375°F), Gas Mark 5. Grease an 18–20 cm (7–8 inch) fluted flan ring on a baking sheet.

2 Sift the flour and cinnamon into a bowl. Rub in the butter until the mixture resembles fine breadcrumbs. Add the sugar, almonds and lemon rind. Bind the dough with the egg yolks and enough lemon juice to make a stiff dough. Turn out on to a floured surface and knead lightly.

3 Roll two-thirds of the dough out and use to line the flan ring. Make sure the dough is evenly rolled out, press to the shape of the ring and trim off the excess. Fill the flan with the raspberry jam. Roll out the reserved dough and trimmings and cut into long strips with a pastry wheel or knife. Use these to make a lattice over the jam.

4 Bake for 25–30 minutes, until golden brown. Allow to cool, then remove the flan ring.

Serves 6

apple strudel

Strudel dough is wafer thin. Make your hand into a fist to stretch the dough over, especially if you have long fingernails that are likely to puncture it. Strudel literally means 'whirlwind'. It is one of the most famous Viennese pastries.

Preparation time: 20 minutes, plus standing
Cooking time: 20–25 minutes

Strudel pastry:
150 g (5 oz) plain flour
pinch of salt
2 teaspoons oil
½ beaten egg
about 125 ml (4 fl oz) lukewarm
  water

Filling:
500 g (1 lb) cooking apples, peeled,
  cored and sliced
50 g (2 oz) currants
50 g (2 oz) sultanas
1 teaspoon ground cinnamon
3 tablespoons breadcrumbs,
  toasted
25 g (1 oz) butter, melted
icing sugar, for dusting

1 Mix the flour with the salt in a large bowl. Make a well in the centre, add the oil, egg and 2–3 tablespoons of the water. Start to mix, adding more warm water if necessary to make a soft paste. Beat, using your hand, until smooth. Cover and leave for 15 minutes, then knead until very smooth.

2 Mix the apples with the currants, sultanas, cinnamon and 1 tablespoon of the breadcrumbs. Heat the oven to 200°C (400°F), Gas Mark 6.

3 Roll out the pastry on a floured surface to 1 cm (½ inch) thickness. Lift on to a floured kitchen towel and leave for 8 minutes. Carefully stretch it until it is very thin. Brush with the butter and sprinkle with the remaining breadcrumbs. Scatter over the fruit and roll up. Place on a greased baking sheet in a horseshoe shape and brush with butter. Bake for 20–25 minutes until golden. Dust with icing sugar and slice to serve.

Serves 6

gâteau pithiviers

This delicious pastry cake originated in Pithiviers in France. It is traditionally served on Twelfth Night when it is called 'Tarte de roi'.

Preparation time: 20 minutes
Cooking time: 35–40 minutes

150 g (5 oz) unsalted butter,
   softened
150 g (5 oz) icing sugar
2 eggs, beaten
2 tablespoons rum
150 g (5 oz) ground almonds
few drops of almond essence
500 g (1 lb) puff pastry, defrosted if
   frozen
1 egg, beaten, to glaze

1 Heat the oven to 220°C (425°F), Gas Mark 7. Grease a baking sheet.

2 Beat the butter in a bowl until creamy. Beat in the icing sugar, then beat for about 5 minutes more, until light and fluffy. Beat in the eggs, a little at a time, then stir in the rum, ground almonds and almond essence.

3 Roll out half the pastry and trim to a 28 cm (11 inch) round, using a plate as a guide. Place on the baking sheet. Spread the filling over the pastry to within 1 cm (½ inch) of the edge. Brush the edge with water.

4 Roll out the remaining pastry to a slightly larger round and cover the pie. Press the edges firmly to seal, then trim the edges, and flute with the back of a knife. With the point of a sharp knife, score the top of the dough from the centre outward, to represent the spokes of a wheel. Do not cut right through to the filling.

5 Brush the top of the pastry with egg, taking care not to brush the sides, as this will stop the dough from rising. Bake for 35–40 minutes until a rich golden brown. Serve warm.

Serves 10–12